PRESIDENT AND PUBLISHER: Patrick J. Purcell
EDITORIAL DIRECTOR: Kenneth A. Chandler
MANAGING EDITOR: Kevin R. Convey
EXECUTIVE SPORTS EDITOR: Mark Torpey
DIRECTOR OF PHOTOGRAPHY: Jim Mahoney
VICE PRESIDENT/PROMOTION: Gwen Gage
CHIEF LIBRARIAN: John Cronin

www.SportsPublishingLLC.com

PUBLISHERS: Peter L. Bannon and Joseph J. Bannon Sr.
SENIOR MANAGING EDITOR: Susan M. Moyer
ACQUISITIONS EDITOR: Joseph J. Bannon Jr.
DEVELOPMENTAL EDITORS: Erin Linden-Levy and Dean Miller
ART DIRECTOR: K. Jeffrey Higgerson
DUST JACKET DESIGN: Joseph T. Brumleve
BOOK LAYOUT: Greg Hickman
IMAGING: Dustin Hubbart
VICE PRESIDENT OF SALES AND MARKETING: Kevin King
MEDIA AND PROMOTIONS MANAGERS: Nick Obradovich (regional),
Randy Fouts (national), Maurey Williamson (print)

Front cover foreground photo by David Goldman/*Boston Herald*
Front cover background photo by Matthew West/*Boston Herald*
Back cover photo by Stuart Cahill/*Boston Herald*

Hard cover ISBN: 1-59670-056-4
Softd cover ISBN: 1-59670-093-9

© 2005 by the *Boston Herald*

Printed in the United States

Sports Publishing L.L.C.
804 North Neil Street
Champaign, IL 61820

Phone: 1-877-424-2665
Fax: 217-363-2073
Web site: www.SportsPublishingLLC.com

CONTENTS

ABOVE: Patriots fans show their team spirit on a cold day at Heinz Field in Pittsburgh.
(Michael Seamans/Boston Herald)

BOSTON HERALD CREDITS

The entire staff of the *Boston Herald* photography department contributed to the coverage of the New England Patriots' 2004-05 season, which culminated in a Super Bowl victory. We gratefully acknowledge the efforts of staff photographers:

Michael Adaskaveg
Tara Bricking
Stuart Cahill
Renee DeKona
Robert Eng
Michael Fein
Ted Fitzgerald
Mark Garfinkel
David Goldman
Jon Hill
Nancy Lane
Douglas McFadd
Faith Ninivaggi
Angela Rowlings
Michael Seamans
Matt Stone
Matthew West
Patrick Whittemore
John Wilcox

Jim Mahoney, Director of Photography
Ted Ancher, Assistant Director
Arthur Pollock, Assistant Director
John Landers, Night Picture Editor

PATS LOSE MEMORY

By Kevin Mannix, *Boston Herald*

The message from the Patriot players was clear: Forget 2003. As nice as the season went for them, with their second Super Bowl championship in three years and the 15 one-game winning streaks that made it possible, it's over. Gone. Finished. Dead and buried. Inconsequential.

"Everybody in the league is 0-0 right now, man," Troy Brown said succinctly.

Pats coach Bill Belichick has been pounding away at that message all through minicamp and the offseason conditioning workouts. Not that it took much persuasion. The majority of the players learned the lesson the hard way—via personal experience—just two years ago. They failed to even qualify for the 2002 playoffs after winning the 2001 championship.

"Coach was talking about how the teams that were in the Super Bowl two years ago didn't even make the playoffs last year," quarterback Tom Brady said. "And three years ago, when it was us and the Rams in the Super Bowl, neither made the playoffs the next year.

"We learned firsthand that just because we played well in one year doesn't mean there will

ABOVE: Defensive back Eugene Wilson defends against Chas Gessner during Patriots training camp.
(Ted Fitzgerald/Boston Herald)

ABOVE: Safety Shawn Mayer sends Chas Gessner to the ground, forcing Gessner to drop the pass.
(Matthew West/Boston Herald)

be a carry-over in the next. And look back at last year. Every game was competitive."

Cornerback Ty Law knows the history of Super Bowl teams the years after their titles. But he also understands that his team didn't collapse in 2002. It just didn't make the playoffs.

"The big lessons from that year is that we need to take advantage of every opportunity starting right away," Law pointed out. "It's not like we went 3-13 like some teams [coming off a championship]. We just missed the playoffs by one game.

"It was a case of too little too late for us back then. That showed us how there is no margin for error and how important it is to get your game going from the beginning because you're the team everybody is gunning for.

"We have a better understanding of that now because this team has a number of veterans who have been through this before."

One of those is Pro Bowl defensive tackle Richard Seymour, who was a rookie first-round draft pick in the 2001 season.

"We just didn't play good enough the year after we won that last championship," Seymour said. "This is a better team than that one. Definitely better when you add in the people we have. But that's just on paper. You have to play better to be better, and how we play remains to be seen."

Complacency after success is human nature, but as linebacker Ted Johnson pointed out, "Sometimes you have to kick human nature in the ass because complacency is always a killer. And I have full confidence that this team will not be complacent at all. We have a coach who demands attention to detail."

BELOW: Head coach Bill Belichick laughs as he makes his rounds during stretching.
(Matt Stone/Boston Herald)

#12 TOM BRADY

Feeling bad about yourself, Bunky? Getting no respect at your job or at home? Looking for some love? Just put on a Patriots jersey and helmet and come down to the team's training camp. You'll become an immediate star of the day.

The thousands of fans who have been jamming the Gillette Stadium facility during the early days of the Pats training camp love their football and their football players even more.

First-year wide receiver Chas Gessner, who has never even played in an NFL game, got a rousing ovation when he caught a pass from Kliff Kingsbury on opening day. It didn't matter that nobody was covering Gessner.

Yesterday, free agent offensive tackle James "Big Cat" Williams was greeted by loud applause as he jogged in front of the bleachers. The fact he was running a lap as punishment for having jumped offside during a practice drill wasn't a problem for the fans. He's a Patriot, so he's a good guy.

That's why there is a loud ovation when the players begin their walk from the stadium to the practice fields.

The loudest applause, naturally enough, is for Tom Brady. Being the quarterback for a championship team, and a two-time Super Bowl MVP to boot, earns you bonus points.

A Brady sighting at any point on the field creates thunderous ovations. When he makes his way from the warmup drills to the end zone, where the quarterbacks loosen up their throwing arms, the place erupts.

"It's Brady," shouted one teenage girl as the quarterback stopped about 100 yards away from her and her fellow fans. "And he's so close. Braaaaaady! Braaaaady! Over here, Tom. Over here."

She and her pals got no response but they shouldn't take it personally.

"You just can't respond when you're out there," the quarterback explained. "As soon as you raise your arms [in response] or wave back, the whole team gives you crap. Like 'Oh, you've got to wave to everybody, huh?' So everybody decides to play it cool, as if they don't hear it. But you hear everything."

And what Brady has been hearing has been exclusively positive. He has succeeded beyond anybody's expectations and people want that to continue. And he can't be made to look bad, as a ballboy learned the other day when he dropped a Brady pass in the corner of the end zone. He got booed. A ballboy! Now that's a tough crowd.

"They're just excited about the season," Brady said. "I remember the first preseason game here two years ago and seeing how the fans supported us last year. We were undefeated at home and a big part of that was because of the support the fans gave us."

That's not likely to change any time soon.

Nor is the role Brady will be playing for this team. Other than head coach Bill Belichick, Brady is the Most Indispensable Person in this organization.

With him at quarterback, this team is a prohibitive favorite to win the AFC East again as well as a solid favorite to become the first team to win consecutive Super Bowls since Denver in 1997 and 1998 and only the fourth team in NFL history to win three championships over a four-year period.

Without him this team would struggle to get above .500. One of the reasons he's been so productive for the past three years has been a devotion to duty.

"He's one of the guys who really sets the pace for everybody else," Belichick said. "That was true after the '01 season. It was true after the '02 season and it was true after last season. In my observation of Tom, he's been as consistent as any player I've ever been around in terms of his work ethic, his preparation and his diligence.

"He's just not working for himself. He's there to work hard to get better to help the team improve. He's working with the other people so he can help improve their games."

And we thought the fans were big Bradyphiles.

—By Kevin Mannix, *Boston Herald*

Position: *Quarterback*
Height: *6'4"*
Weight: *225*
Born: *8/3/77*
College: *Michigan*
NFL Experience: *5 years*

Nancy Lane/Boston Herald

PATRIOTS START WILD RIDE

By Michael Felger, *Boston Herald*

I t was a star-studded opening night unlike any other in the history of New England sports. It was a result that everyone has come to expect from the New England Patriots.

The Pats began their Super Bowl title defense in dramatic style, defeating the Indianapolis Colts, 27-24, on the strength of another rousing goal-line stand by the defense and an uncharacteristic miss from the most accurate field goal kicker in the history of the NFL, the Colts' Mike Vanderjagt.

"I didn't choke," Vanderjagt said. "I didn't feel the pressure. It didn't go in. I'm not perfect anymore, I guess."

That last-ditch effort by the Colts came some four hours after Toby Keith, Lenny Kravitz and the unveiling of the Pats' 2003 championship banner put the crowd of 68,756 into a frenzy. But as Willie McGinest said, "Our show was more entertaining."

No question about that, and just like in the Pats' dramatic victory in Indianapolis last November, McGinest provided the key play last night when his 12-yard sack of Peyton Manning

ABOVE: Corey Dillon breaks free for a long, third-quarter run to put the Pats in position for a touchdown. Dillon rushed for 86 yards against the Colts. *(Michael Seamans/Boston Herald)*

ABOVE: Anthony Floyd can't catch up as David Patten hauls in a 25-yard touchdown pass in the third quarter. *(Michael Seamans/Boston Herald)*

in the closing seconds put Vanderjagt into a long-range situation (48 yards) facing the wind.

Still, given Vanderjagt's history—he had made a record 42 straight kicks—the Pats assumed the game would be tied. Pats kicker Adam Vinatieri was so sure his counterpart would make it he wasn't even watching. Vinatieri was warming up into the net, anticipating overtime.

But Vanderjagt's kick sailed wide right and the Pats had their 16th consecutive victory (including playoffs). They are now just two wins away from tying the unofficial NFL record.

The Colts probably should have won the game, and they had several opportunities to do so. The most obvious chance came with just under four minutes remaining in the game. But after a fumbled punt by Deion Branch and a marginal pass interference call on Asante Samuel gave the Colts first-and-goal at the Pats' 1, Eugene Wilson and rookie Vince Wilfork forced an Edgerrin James fumble on the goal line to preserve the lead.

"That's what champions do. They survive," Wilson said. "We just collapsed on him. I didn't know it popped out. I just turned around and saw the big man [Wilfork] running with the ball."

Added Wilfork, who drew the surprise start at nose tackle: "From the block they gave me, I knew exactly what they were trying to run. So, one good play in many to come in my career."

Meanwhile, quarterback Tom Brady was outstanding, throwing for 335 yards and three touchdowns. His only mistake was a fourth-quarter interception. Brady's third-quarter touchdown passes to David Patten and Daniel Graham erased a 17-13 halftime deficit and gave the Pats the cushion for the fourth quarter.

The Pats also debuted new running back Corey Dillon, and he made several eye-opening gains in rushing for 86 yards on 15 carries. However, Dillon didn't get the ball nearly

	1st	2nd	3rd	4th	Final
Indianapolis	0	17	0	7	24
New England	3	10	14	0	27

Scoring Summary
New England Adam Vinatieri 32-yard field goal. Nine plays, 48 yards in 4:51.
Indianapolis Mike Vanderjagt 32-yard field goal. Ten plays, 49 yards in 4:05.
Indianapolis Dominic Rhodes three-yard run (Vanderjagt kick). Nine plays, 66 yards in 4:12.
New England Deion Branch 16-yard pass from Tom Brady (Vinatieri kick). Eight plays, 75 yards in 4:58.
Indianapolis Marvin Harrison three-yard pass from Peyton Manning (Vanderjagt kick). Seven plays, 82 yards in 2:22.
New England Adam Vinatieri 43-yard field goal. Six plays, 34 yards in 0:42.
New England David Patten 25-yard pass from Tom Brady (Vinatieri kick). Seven plays, 69 yards in 3:01.
New England Daniel Graham eight-yard pass from Tom Brady (Vinatieri kick). Seven plays, 82 yards in 3:43.
Indianapolis Brandon Stokley seven-yard pass from Peyton Manning (Vanderjagt kick). Eleven plays, 74 yards in 5:18.

Team Statistics
Category	Indianapolis	New England
First Downs	28	22
Rushes-Yards (Net)	42-202	17-82
Passing-Yards (Net)	244	320
Passes Att-Comp-Int	29-16-1	38-26-1
Total Offense Plays-Yards	72-446	57-402
Punt Returns-Yards	2-20	2-6
Kickoff Returns-Yards	4-89	5-107
Punts (Number-Avg)	2-41.0	3-47.3
Fumbles-Lost	2-2	2-1
Penalties-Yards	3-20	8-55
Possession Time	31:41	28:19
Sacks by (Number-Yards)	2-15	1-12

Individual Offensive Statistics
Rushing: **Indianapolis** E. James 30-142; D. Rhodes 10-42; P. Manning 2-18
New England C. Dillon 15-86; T. Brady 1-minus 1; B. Johnson 1-minus 3

Passing: **Indianapolis** P. Manning 16-29-2-256
New England T. Brady 26-38-3-335

Receiving: **Indianapolis** B. Stokley 4-77; D. Clark 1-64; M. Harrison 7-44; R. Wayne 1-42; E. James 3-29
New England D. Branch 7-86; D. Patten 4-86; D. Givens 4-80; D. Graham 7-57; B. Watson 2-16; C. Fauria 1-5; B. Johnson 1-5

Individual Defensive Statistics
Interceptions: **Indianapolis** N. Harper 1
New England T. Bruschi 1

Sacks: **Indianapolis** R. Brock 1; D. Freeney 1
New England W. McGinest 1

Tackles (unassisted-assisted): **Indianapolis** D. Strickland 7-1; R. Morris 5-0; A. Floyd 4-3; N. Harper 4-1; J. Nelson 4-1; D. Thornton 4-1; R. Brock 2-1; J. David 2-0; D. Freeney 2-0; C. June 2-2; M. Reagor 2-1
New England R. Phifer 8-6; E. Wilson 6-1; T. Bruschi 5-7; T. Warren 5-1; W. McGinest 4-2; R. Harrison 3-4; L. Izzo 3-0; T. Johnson 3-2; T. Poole 3-0; A. Samuel 3-0; K. Traylor 3-0; M. Vrabel 3-1; S. Mayer 2-0; R. Seymour 2-2; V. Wilfork 2-2

enough in the fourth quarter, and offensive coordinator Charlie Weis will certainly hear about that.

There were other issues for the Pats, most notably their run defense—the Colts ran roughshod for 202 yards on the night—and the microscope their defensive secondary will be under from the officials this season.

But, in the end, the Pats once again made the plays they had to, and Manning (0-6 in Foxboro) and the Colts didn't.

"All the glamour, all the lights," Tedy Bruschi said. "I hope the fans had a good time."

They most certainly did.

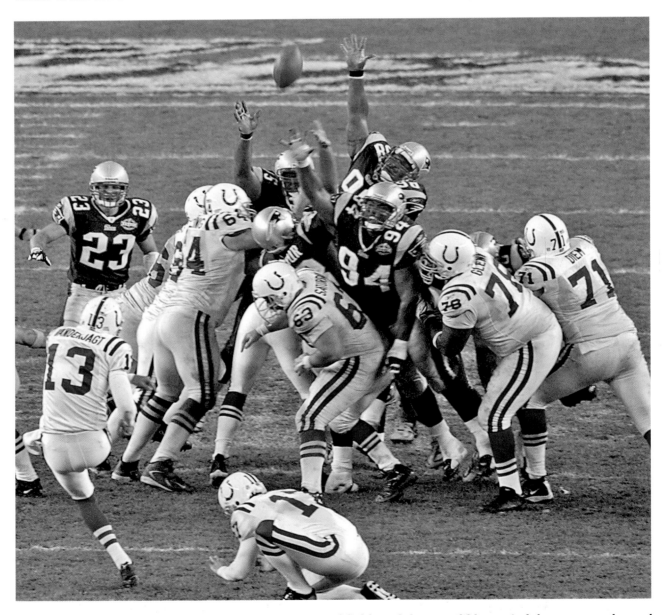

ABOVE: Colts kicker Mike Vanderjagt misses a 48-yard field goal that would have tied the game at the end of the fourth quarter. The Colts lost to the Patriots, 27-24. *(David Goldman/Boston Herald)*

ABOVE: Tom Brady gets a pass off just before Dwight Freeney swarms from behind. Brady completed 26 of 38 passes. *(Michael Seamans/Boston Herald)*

STREAK ROLLS ON

By Michael Felger, *Boston Herald*

The Patriots may be closing on the one-year anniversary of the last time they lost a football game, but that didn't change the mood inside the visitors locker room at Sun Devil Stadium.

The Pats had just secured their 17th consecutive victory with a 23-12 win over woeful Arizona, and many key veterans weren't happy about it. They saw a game that should have been a blowout turn into a tight second-half affair only because of their own sloppiness and ineffectiveness.

"We should have buried them, and we didn't do it," said captain Rodney Harrison. "We make it tough on ourselves. When we have the chance to blow somebody out, you've got to do it. We can't keep playing like this. We can't keep making it close like this. Because, in the end, our luck is going to run out."

"The end result is we finished the way we wanted to, but we have to eliminate the penalties and the turnovers and become a better team," said linebacker Willie McGinest. "We did all right. We made a little improvement, but we can always get better. We will get better."

ABOVE: Wide receiver David Givens gives Cardinals cornerback Duane Sharks the slip in the fourth quarter. *(Matthew West/Boston Herald)*

ABOVE: Rodney Harrison (37) and Willie McGinest (55) sack Cardinals quarterback Josh McCown.
(Matthew West/Boston Herald)

Publicly at least, coach Bill Belichick wasn't as harsh.

"As usual, it was a dogfight," said Belichick. "Offensively, we hurt ourselves with turnovers and touchdowns called back. Defensively, we played with a little more intensity than last week [against the Colts]. We're happy to win, but we still have a lot to do. There's no question about that."

The Pats were sharp early, taking a 14-point lead on a pair of Daniel Graham touchdown catches in the first half. But from there the game was even, as the teams traded turnovers and sloppy play. Corey Dillon was the horse while receiver David Givens was a second-half catalyst.

The defense also stepped up with some more inspired play, and the unit made life miserable for quarterback Josh McCown. Given all those factors, the Pats should have walked away with an easy win. But true to form, the Pats made it difficult on themselves. If not for three field goals from Adam Vinatieri, the outcome would have been worse.

Regardless, the players probably weren't going to talk about their winning streak. But when the questions came after a mediocre performance, their answers were almost predictable.

A 17-game winning streak? What 17-game winning streak?

	1st	2nd	3rd	4th	Final
New England	7	7	3	6	23
Arizona	0	6	6	0	12

Scoring Summary

New England Daniel Graham two-yard pass from Tom Brady (Vinatieri kick). Eight plays, 68 yards in 5:15.
New England Daniel Graham 19-yard pass from Tom Brady (Vinatieri kick). Five plays, 30 yards in 2:27.
Arizona Neil Rackers 51-yard field goal. Four plays, -22 yards in 1:54.
Arizona Neil Rackers 52-yard field goal. Four plays, eight yards in 2:04.
New England Adam Vinatieri 29-yard field goal. Twelve plays, 69 yards in 5:39.
Arizona Emmitt Smith, one-yard run (McCown pass failed). Eleven plays, 80 yards in 7:48.
New England Adam Vinatieri 28-yard field goal. Nine plays, 69 yards in 4:31.
New England Adam Vinatieri 24-yard field goal. Seven plays, 42 yards in 3:56.

Team Statistics

Category	New England	Arizona
First Downs	24	14
Rushes-Yards (Net)	42-172	16-50
Passing-Yards (Net)	205	117
Passes Att-Comp-Int	26-15-2	29-13-2
Total Offense Plays-Yards	70-377	50-167
Punt Returns-Yards	4-27	0-0
Kickoff Returns-Yards	1-23	5-108
Punts (Number-Avg)	3-45.7	4-45.0
Fumbles-Lost	2-1	3-0
Penalties-Yards	12-79	6-43
Possession Time	35:16	24:44
Sacks by (Number-Yards)	5-43	2-12

Individual Offensive Statistics

Rushing: **New England** C. Dillon 32-158; P. Pass 4-7; R. Abdullah 1-4; T. Brady 5-3
Arizona E. Smith 13-31; J. McCown 3-19

Passing: **New England** T. Brady 15-26-2-217
Arizona J. McCown 13-29-0-160

Receiving: **New England** D. Givens 6-118; D. Patten 2-39; P. Pass 2-27; D. Graham 2-21; D. Branch 1-7; T. Brown 1-6; C. Dillon 1-minus 1
Arizona F. Jones 4-43; J. Scobey 1-42; B. Johnson 3-39; L. Fitzgerald 5-36

Individual Defensive Statistics

Interceptions: **New England** E. Wilson 2
Arizona J. Darling 1; D. Macklin 1

Sacks: **New England** R. Harrison 2; W. McGinest 2; M. Vrabel 1
Arizona B. Berry 1; R. Kolodziej 1

Tackles (unassisted-assisted): **New England** R. Harrison 7-0; T. Law 5-0; W. McGinest 3-1; M. Vrabel 3-0; E. Wilson 3-0; R. Phifer 2-0; T. Poole 2-0; A. Samuel 2-0; V. Wilfork 2-0.
Arizona A. Wilson 10-1; J. Darling 6-3; D. Macklin 6-0; R. Tate 6-0; B. Berry 5-2; R. Davis 5-1; Q. Harris 5-1; K. Dansby 3-1; D. Carter 2-0; D. Dockett 2-0; R. Kolodziej 2-0; D. Starks 2-0; L. Woods 2-3

PATS TIE WIN STREAK

By Michael Felger, *Boston Herald*

The special teams were as shaky as they've ever been under Bill Belichick. Drew Bledsoe actually was allowed to make a few plays, and the Patriots made enough mistakes to keep the projection screens lit up all afternoon today when the players convene back at Gillette Stadium.

In the end, however, none of it mattered, just like it hasn't mattered since September 28, 2003.

That's the last time the Patriots lost a football game, and with the 31-17 triumph against the Buffalo Bills they tied the unofficial NFL record of consecutive victories with 18. Of course, it was a record no one in the Pats locker room would talk about. In fact, few people even asked the question.

Instead, the big question was: How do the Pats keep doing it?

"We made the crucial plays at the crucial times to get the win, and that's what this team is about," said Richard Seymour, whose 68-yard return of a Bledsoe fumble for a touchdown was the game's epitaph. "We make plays when the pressure is on. We have an attitude that we can't

ABOVE: Corey Dillon celebrates his first-quarter touchdown with Tom Brady and Matt Light.
(Nancy Lane/Boston Herald)

ABOVE: Tom Brady passes downfield in the first quarter. Brady connected with receivers 17 times for two touchdowns. *(Nancy Lane/Boston Herald)*

be denied and that we won't lose. That's just our attitude."

A loss seemed a distinct possibility in the first half, as Bledsoe opened the game with a 55-yard bomb and later hit Eric Moulds for a pretty, 41-yard score. The Pats also committed seven penalties in the half and put forth enough sloppy play to receive an attitude adjustment at halftime.

It worked. Belichick said his players had better "focus" after the intermission and coordinators Romeo Crennel and Charlie Weis deserved credit for making the right adjustments, the most important of which was taking away the deep ball from Bledsoe.

"That's the only way they were going to beat us—with the big play," safety Rodney Harrison said. "We knew they couldn't move the ball down the field on us and win."

It turns out the Bills couldn't, and the Pats defense forced Bledsoe to hold the ball and look for shorter, more patient options.

So just what was said at the half?

"Stop shooting ourselves in the foot," Harrison said.

Added linebacker Mike Vrabel: "We eliminated mistakes. We eliminated the penalties. We came out and played better football, and that was it."

Meanwhile, Tom Brady took advantage of a Buffalo secondary that lost starting cornerback Troy Vincent (knee) on the first series and was without safety Lawyer Milloy (forearm). The result was several huge plays—most on third down—and a 298-yard, two-touchdown afternoon for the Pats quarterback.

The Bills tried to blitz Brady on nearly every play, and they paid a heavy price. Brady's 30-yard pass to a wide-open David Patten tied the game at 17 late in the second quarter, and his two-yard pass to Daniel Graham with 11:17 left in the fourth quarter proved the difference.

Special teams nearly killed the Pats. In the first quarter, they allowed a 98-yard kickoff

	1st	2nd	3rd	4th	Final
New England	10	7	0	14	31
Buffalo	10	7	0	0	17

Scoring Summary

New England Corey Dillon 15-yard run (Vinatieri kick) Nine plays, 77 yards in 4:49.

Buffalo Rian Lindell 33-yard field goal. Seven plays, 66 yards in 3:52.

New England Adam Vinatieri 42-yard field goal. Ten plays, 56 yards in 4:39.

Buffalo Terrence McGee 98-yard kick return (Lindell kick).

Buffalo Eric Moulds 41-yard pass from Drew Bledsoe (Lindell kick). Six plays, 96 yards in 2:54.

New England David Patten 30-yard pass from Tom Brady (Vinatieri kick). Six plays, 61 yards in 1:15.

New England Daniel Graham two-yard pass from Tom Brady (Vinatieri kick). Twelve plays, 80 yards in 5:57.

New England Richard Seymour 68-yard fumble return (Vinatieri kick).

Team Statistics

Category	New England	Buffalo
First Downs	21	18
Rushes-Yards (Net)	26-99	26-138
Passing-Yards (Net)	298	199
Passes Att-Comp-Int	30-17-0	30-18-1
Total Offense Plays-Yards	56-397	63-337
Punt Returns-Yards	1-0	2-22
Kickoff Returns-Yards	4-96	5-191
Punts (Number-Avg)	4-49.5	5-51.2
Fumbles-Lost	2-1	2-1
Penalties-Yards	10-77	11-94
Possession Time	28:43	31:17
Sacks by (Number-Yards)	7-48	0-0

Individual Offensive Statistics

Rushing: **New England** C. Dillon 19-79; P. Pass 5-18; T. Brady 2-2
Buffalo T. Henry 24-98; B. Moorman 1-34; J. Reed 1-6; J. Dorenbos 1-0

Passing: **New England** T. Brady 17-30-2-298
Buffalo D. Bledsoe 18-30-1-247

Receiving: **New England** D. Patten 5-113; D. Givens 4-86; D. Graham 2-35; C. Fauria 2-24; C. Dillon 3-23; B. Johnson 1-17
Buffalo E. Moulds 10-126; L. Evans 4-93; S. Aiken 2-12; T. Henry 1-10; R. Neufeld 1-6

Individual Defensive Statistics

Interceptions: **New England** T. Poole 1
Buffalo none

Sacks: **New England** d T. Bruschi 2; M. Vrabel 1; R. Colvin 1; R. Seymour 1; R. Phifer 1; V. Wilfork 1
Buffalo none

Tackles (unassisted-assisted): **New England** M. Vrabel 7-0; T. Johnson 5-0; T. Poole 5-0; E. Wilson 5-0; T. Bruschi 4-3; R. Colvin 3-1; R. Harrison 3-2; T. Law 3-0; R. Seymour 3-0; T. Warren 3-1; D. Davis 2-0; L. Izzo 2-0; P. Pass 2-0; R. Phifer 2-0; K. Traylor 2-1
Buffalo L. Fletcher 7-2; T. McGee 6-1; T. Spikes 5-4; N. Clements 3-0; C. Wire 3-1; J. Posey 2-1; P. Prioleau 2-0; I. Reese 2-3

BELOW: Rodney Harrison, Ted Johnson (52) and Tedy Bruschi (54) celebrate Drew Bledsoe's incomplete pass to Ryan Neufeld (88). *(Nancy Lane/Boston Herald)*

ABOVE: David Givens makes a 44-yard, over-the-shoulder catch in the first quarter with Coy Wire hot on his heels. *(Nancy Lane/Boston Herald)*

return for a touchdown by Terrence McGee. In the second, they allowed punter Brian Moorman to pick up a flubbed snap and run 49 yards for a first down (Bledsoe hit Moulds for a score on the next play). In the third, Tyrone Poole muffed a punt that put the Pats back at their three-yard line.

The Pats, however, overcame once again.

"When our backs are to the wall, that's when we feel most comfortable, because we trust ourselves and we trust our coaches," cornerback Ty Law said. "We look at all 11 guys and know we can get it done."

ROOKIES PICK UP SLACK

By Rich Thompson, *Boston Herald*

The Patriots secondary was the primary source of favorable field position for the offense in the 24-10 victory over the Miami Dolphins at Gillette Stadium.

Quarterback Tom Brady converted a pair of Miami turnovers into 14 points, courtesy of big plays by rookies Randall Gay (interception) and Dexter Reid (fumble recovery).

First-year nose tackle Vince Wilfork also did his part with seven tackles and a sack. The first-round pick out of Miami also tipped a pass on the Dolphins' second possession.

"That's why they are here," veteran strong safety Rodney Harrison said. "After training camp we said to those guys they aren't rookies anymore because they are ready to play.

"We had Tyrone Poole go down and Randall stepped up and played. Randall is one of those guys…he understands what it means to be a professional and each week he's getting better. Vince and Dexter are young guys that understand the importance of being consistent."

Gay was pressed into service when Poole, the starting right cornerback, couldn't practice due to a knee injury. Gay made the biggest play

ABOVE: Rookie nose tackle Vince Wilfork gets a pat on the head from Keith Taylor after Wilfork sacked Jay Fiedler. *(Nancy Lane/Boston Herald)*

ABOVE: Randall Gay (21) and Dexter Reid (42), both rookies, race up the field after Gay intercepted a pass from Fiedler in the first quarter. *(Nancy Lane/Boston Herald)*

of his career when he picked off a Jay Fiedler pass on the Miami 40 and returned it 10 yards to the 30. Seven plays later, Brady hit tight end Daniel Graham with a one-yard TD pass to make it 7-0.

"[Gay] stepped up and made a big play, and we are going to need more of them," veteran Pro Bowl cornerback Ty Law said. "To go on the field with this team and this defense, you have to have some talent.

"He still has a lot to learn, of course. A rookie is a rookie. But hey, we trust him, and that's why he's out there and that's why I like playing with him."

A combination of factors needed to fall into place for Reid to make the most significant contribution to the Pats' 19-game winning streak. Reid lined up deep in prevent coverage, but the pressure up front was so intense it forced Fiedler to scramble from the pocket.

Harrison caught Fiedler from behind and knocked the ball to the turf. Reid reacted immediately and recovered the loose ball on Miami's 48. Seven plays later, reserve tailback Rabih Abdullah punched it in from the one to give the Pats a 24-7 lead.

"I just happened to be running to the ball and got to the right place at the right time," Reid said. "I give all the credit to Rodney for causing the fumble and I was in the vicinity to fall on the ball."

	1st	2nd	3rd	4th	Final
Miami	0	7	3	0	10
New England	7	10	7	0	24

Scoring Summary
New England Daniel Graham one-yard pass from Tom Brady (Vinatieri kick). Seven plays, 30 yards in 3:30.
New England Adam Vinatieri 40-yard field goal. Ten plays, 42 yards in 4:40.
Miami Chris Chambers 10-yard pass from Jay Fiedler (Welker kick). Seven plays, 63 yards in 4:03.
New England David Givens five-yard pass from Tom Brady (Vinatieri kick). Six plays, 46 yards in 2:39.
New England Rabih Abdullah one-yard run (Vinatieri kick). Six plays, 48 yards in 3:18.
Miami Wes Welker 29-yard field goal. Twelve plays, 51 yards in 6:28.

Team Statistics
Category	Miami	New England
First Downs	18	14
Rushes-Yards (Net)	26-67	38-135
Passing-Yards (Net)	228	69
Passes Att-Comp-Int	43-21-1	19-7-1
Total Offense Plays-Yards	72-295	58-204
Punt Returns-Yards	5-41	2-13
Kickoff Returns-Yards	5-101	2-40
Punts (Number-Avg)	3-40.0	5-43.2
Fumbles-Lost	3-1	0-0
Penalties-Yards	12-86	7-55
Possession Time	31:02	28:58
Sacks by (Number-Yards)	1-7	3-29

Individual Offensive Statistics
Rushing: **Miami** B. Forsey 13-44; L. Henry 5-10; S. Morris 3-7; J. Fiedler 3-6; M. Turk 1-3; C. Chambers 1-minus 3
New England C. Dillon 18-94; P. Pass 10-37; R. Abdullah 5-4; K. Faulk 1-1; T. Brady 4-minus 1

Passing: **Miami** J. Fiedler 20-41-1-251; A. Feeley 1-2-0-6
New England T. Brady 7-19-2-76

Receiving: **Miami** M. Booker 7-123; R. McMichael 4-62; C. Chambers 6-37; D. Thompson 2-23; B. Gilmore 1-11; R. Konrad 1-1
New England D. Givens 4-33; D. Patten 1-28; K. Faulk 1-14; D. Graham 1-1

Individual Defensive Statistics
Interceptions: **Miami** P. Surtain 1
New England R. Gay 1

Sacks: **Miami** D. Romero 1
New England R. Harrison 1; V. Wilfork 1; R. Seymour 1

Tackles (unassisted-assisted): **Miami** Z. Thomas 7-1; J. Seau 5-2; M. Greenwood 4-4; S. Knight 4-3; S. Madison 4-1; J. Zgonina 4-1; P. Surtain 3-0; A. Edwards 2-1; D. Romero 2-1; J. Taylor 2-1
New England R. Harrison 7-4; T. Law 7-2; T. Johnson 5-2; V. Wilfork 5-2; P. Pass 4-0; A. Samuel 4-0; T. Bruschi 3-2; L. Izzo 3-0; R. Phifer 3-1; E. Wilson 3-2; K. Traylor 2-0

PATS WIN 20

By Michael Felger, *Boston Herald*

Doesn't the rest of the NFL know by now? Anything you say can, and will, be used against you by the Patriots.

The Seattle Seahawks learned that lesson the hard way. Coach Mike Holmgren allowed his players to talk big during the week, and, as usual, it was the Patriots who had the final word.

The Pats rolled to their 20th consecutive victory—tying the official NFL record of 17 straight regular-season wins—by shutting down, and shutting up, the vaunted Seattle offense when it counted.

The Pats certainly didn't have to work hard for their motivation. It was there in black and white, as Seahawks receiver Darrell Jackson said the Pats were "beatable. I don't really think they're that good."

Bill Belichick's staff made sure the players saw that quote, as well as others that mentioned the age of the defense. And safety Rodney Harrison certainly remembered a confrontation with Matt Hasselbeck at the end of a game in 2002, when the Seattle quarterback told the

ABOVE: Pats fans hold up "20" signs, signifying the number of consecutive Patriots victories, as the Patriots take on the Seattle Seahawks. (*Stuart Cahill/Boston Herald*)

ABOVE: Bethel Johnson flattens out to catch a 48-yard pass from Brady and make the first down for the Patriots. *(Stuart Cahill/Boston Herald)*

then-San Diego safety, "My grandmother hits harder than that."

"We handed out a little bit of humble pie today—and we told them that," said cornerback Ty Law. "The one that stuck out in my mind was [the comment] that said we were old. Well, this old man had to show you something."

Harrison saved most of his vengeance for Jackson, who had just two catches.

"Having to take all that talk, we were ready," said Harrison. "All game I was in [Jackson's] ear. I was like, 'You're not doing anything today.' I just said, 'Hey, this isn't a mistake, man. This is 20 in a row for us. You've got to start respecting it. You earn your respect right here.' And he shut up. What can you say when you have two catches?"

The Pats certainly came out on fire, bolting out to first-half leads of 17-0 and 20-6. Seattle got its legs in the second half, and after Tom Brady committed a pair of uncharacteristic fourth-quarter turnovers (fumble, interception) the Seahawks closed the gap to 23-20.

That's when the Pats came up with a typical big play using typically unsung personnel. After being benched one week earlier against Miami, receiver Bethel Johnson made a beautiful diving catch of a 48-yard Brady bomb to bail the Pats out of a third-and-seven situation. Two plays later, Corey Dillon scored his second touchdown of the day on a nine-yard run to seal the deal.

"He did what he was supposed to do," said Belichick of Johnson, who was held out of a victory at Gillette against the Dolphins, in part, because of his reluctance to learn new plays. "We always tell [Brady] to throw it up there—you can't overthrow him. And he almost did."

Meanwhile, Dillon shook off a sore foot to rush for 105 yards. He knew his relatives were watching back home in Seattle, but Dillon seemed to be more happy to shut up the Seahawks.

	1st	2nd	3rd	4th	Final
Seattle	0	6	3	11	20
New England	10	10	0	10	30

Scoring Summary

New England Corey Dillon one-yard run (Vinatieri kick). Five plays, 26 yards in 2:22.
New England Adam Vinatieri 40-yard field goal. Seven plays, 21 yards in 2:48.
New England David Patten six-yard pass from Tom Brady (Vinatieri kick). Six plays, 67 yards in 3:07.
Seattle Josh Brown 33-yard field goal. Eight plays, 59 yards in 2:57.
New England Adam Vinatieri 39-yard field goal. Twelve plays, 50 yards in 6:28.
Seattle Josh Brown 40-yard field goal. Ten plays, 41 yards in 2:33.
Seattle Josh Brown 28-yard field goal. Eleven plays, 73 yards in 4:12.
Seattle Shaun Alexander nine-yard run (Stevens pass from Hasselbeck). Four plays, 45 yards in 1:32.
New England Adam Vinatieri 30-yard field goal. Twelve plays, 68 yards in 4:22.
Seattle Josh Brown 31-yard field goal. Eleven plays, 62 yards in 3:42.
New England Corey Dillon nine-yard run (Vinatieri kick). Five plays, 63 yards in 1:06.

Team Statistics

Category	Seattle	New England
First Downs	23	20
Rushes-Yards (Net)	21-102	33-138
Passing-Yards (Net)	341	224
Passes Att-Comp-Int	50-27-2	30-19-1
Total Offense Plays-Yards	74-443	64-362
Punt Returns-Yards	1-0	2-15
Kickoff Returns-Yards	7-171	5-118
Punts (Number-Avg)	3-38.0	2-40.5
Fumbles-Lost	1-0	1-1
Penalties-Yards	6-50	6-46
Possession Time	28:23	31:37
Sacks by (Number-Yards)	1-7	3-8

Individual Offensive Statistics

Rushing: Seattle S. Alexander 16-77; M. Morris 2-16; M. Strong 3-9
New England C. Dillon 23-105; K. Faulk 6-21; T. Brady 3-7; D. Patten 1-5

Passing: Seattle M. Hasselbeck 27-50-0-349
New England T. Brady 19-30-1-231

Receiving: Seattle K. Robinson 9-150; J. Stevens 4-50; D. Jackson 2-40; B. Engram 3-35; S. Alexander 2-30; I. Mili 1-17; A. Bannister 2-10; M. Strong 3-10; M. Morris 1-7
New England D. Patten 5-58; B. Johnson 1-48; D. Graham 4-45; K. Faulk 4-37; D. Givens 1-17; D. Klecko 1-11; R. Abdullah 1-9; C. Dillon 2-6

Individual Defensive Statistics

Interceptions: Seattle M. Boulware 1
New England T. Law 1; W. McGinest 1

Sacks (unassisted-assisted): Seattle C. Okeafor 1
New England M. Vrabel 1; J. Green 1; T. Warren 1

Tackles (unassisted-assisted): Seattle K. Lucas 8-1; T. Bierria 7-3; I. Kacyvenski 6-3; K. Hamlin 4-2; A. Simmons 4-2; G. Wistrom 4-2; O. Huff 3-1; T. White 3-1; R. Bernard 2-0; A. Cochran 2-0; C. Okeafor 2-2; M. Trufant 2-0
New England E. Wilson 10-0; T. Bruschi 6-2; R. Harrison 6-6; M. Vrabel 5-2; T. Law 4-1; A. Samuel 4-0; J. Cherry 3-0; R. Phifer 3-0; J. Green 2-0; D. Klecko 2-0

"It was [satisfying] due to the fact they were talking a lot," said Dillon. "It was nice to take care of that. We sent them off with a nice message."

Defensively, the Pats were able to take the Seahawks out of their rhythm in the first half by jamming receivers off their routes (legally, according to Seattle coach Mike Holmgren). Hasselbeck wound up throwing for 349 yards, but he was also sacked three times and intercepted twice.

Most importantly, Seattle scored touchdowns on just 1-of-5 trips inside the red zone.

Law said at least some Seattle players eventually gave the Pats their due.

"They congratulated us after the win," Law said. "They said, 'You guys are pretty good.'"

You think?

BELOW: Tom Brady takes a hard hit from Seattle's Chike Okeafor, forcing an uncharacteristic fumble in the fourth quarter. *(Stuart Cahill/Boston Herald)*

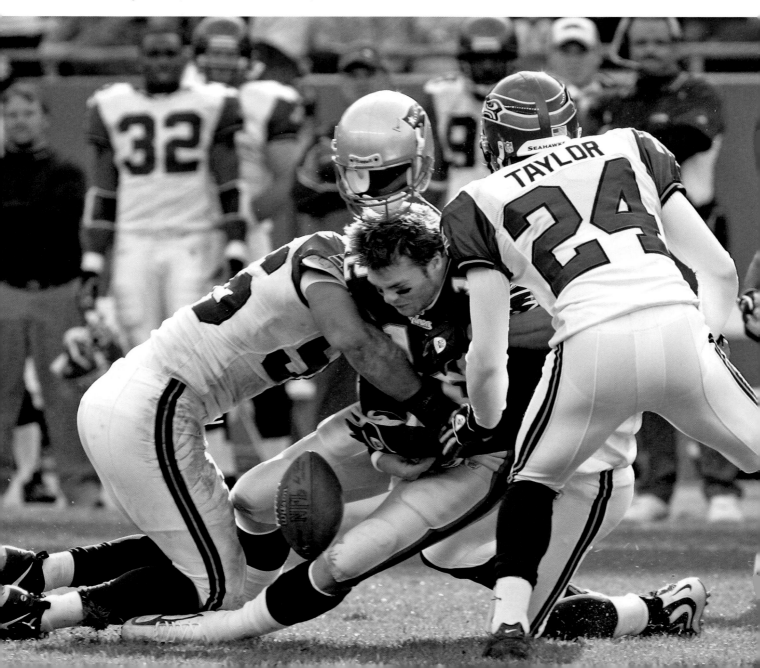

BELOW: David Patten is congratulated by teammate Matt Light after Patten's short touchdown reception in the second quarter. Patten hauled in five passes for 58 yards against the Seahawks. *(Stuart Cahill/Boston Herald)*

GIVENS STEPS UP

By Rich Thompson, *Boston Herald*

The wide receivers have been the most significant contributors to the Patriots' inactive list this season.

Every week quarterback Tom Brady counts on one of his receivers to fill the void created by prolonged injuries to starters Troy Brown and Deion Branch. In the 13-7 victory over the New York Jets, wide receiver David Givens was the man that made the difference.

Givens enjoyed the finest outing of his career in terms of yards gained on the day the Patriots broke the NFL record for consecutive regular-season victories (18). He caught five passes for 107 yards, including a 42-yard strike from Brady.

"We've had some injured guys for a few weeks now, so I think our receiving corps has been stepping up every week," said Givens, whose previous high was an 87-yard effort at Denver last season. "We are 6-0 and it just shows we come out to play every play and every week. I definitely think this could have been one of my best, and Tom did a great job finding the open guys, and he found me a few

ABOVE: David Givens celebrates his long catch deep into Jets territory. Givens had five receptions for 107 yards. *(Michael Seamans/Boston Herald)*

BELOW: Eugene Wilson (26) and Asante Samuel break up a pass to Justin McCareins in the end zone on third down late in the game. *(Michael Seamans/Boston Herald)*

times and I tried to capitalize on my opportunities."

The Patriots opened the second quarter leading by a slim 3-0 margin and were anxious to add to that advantage in what figured to be a close game. Brady was effective moving the chains by using all his receivers on select short routes. Then, on second-and-10 from the Patriots' 48, Brady isolated Givens on Jets right cornerback David Barrett down the left sideline. Givens was able to get separation from Barrett and hauled in the 42-yard bomb at the Jets 10.

The Patriots didn't reach the end zone, but they were able to take a 6-0 lead when Adam Vinatieri booted a 27-yard field goal with 9:35 to play in the half.

"It was a two-man route with the tight end and myself, and basically Tom just picked who was either more open or who he wanted to throw to," Givens said. "We have guys that know how to get open, and Tom does a good job of finding us.

"The coaches make up a great game plan and I just try to make the catches that come my way. I try to take pride in making yards after the catch."

"David made some big plays, especially that big catch he had down the sidelines," Belichick said. "He really went up for it aggressively and went for the ball. Tom hit him and he took a couple of shots there.

"David stepped up. We needed a lot of guys to make big plays today and he was certainly one of them."

	1st	2nd	3rd	4th	Final
New York	0	7	0	0	7
New England	3	10	0	0	13

Scoring Summary
New England Adam Vinatieri 41-yard field goal. Twelve plays, 53 yards in 6:27.
New England Adam Vinatieri 27-yard field goal. Fourteen plays, 84 yards in 7:34.
New York Chad Pennington one-yard run (Brien kick). Thirteen plays, 78 yards in 7:36.
New England David Patten seven-yard pass from Tom Brady (Vinatieri kick). Seven plays, 62 yards in 1:50.

Team Statistics
Category	New York	New England
First Downs	15	21
Rushes-Yards (Net)	27-106	29-133
Passing-Yards (Net)	162	210
Passes Att-Comp-Int	30-19-0	29-20-0
Total Offense Plays-Yards	57-268	61-343
Punt Returns-Yards	1-5	2-3
Kickoff Returns-Yards	4-66	2-46
Punts (Number-Avg)	4-33.8	3-36.7
Fumbles-Lost	2-1	1-1
Penalties-Yards	6-37	6-53
Possession Time	31:01	28:59
Sacks by (Number-Yards)	3-20	0-0

Individual Offensive Statistics
Rushing: **New York** C. Martin 20-70; L. Jordan 3-21; C. Pennington 3-15; S. Moss 1-0
New England C. Dillon 22-115; K. Faulk 4-21; T. Brady 3-minus 3

Passing: **New York** C. Pennington 19-30-0-162
New England T. Brady 20-29-1-230

Receiving: **New York** J. McCareins 6-83; C. Baker 3-26; W. Chrebet 1-18; J. Sowell 2-13; S. Moss 2-12; A. Becht 2-8; L. Jordan 1-2; C. Martin 2-0
New England D. Givens 5-107; K. Faulk 6-44; D. Patten 3-33; D. Graham 2-21; B. Johnson 2-18; D. Klecko 2-7

Individual Defensive Statistics
Interceptions: **New York** none
New England none

Sacks: **New York** D. Robertson 1; S. Ellis 1
New England none

Tackles (unassisted-assisted): **New York** E. Coleman 8-4; D. Barrett 6-2; E. Barton 6-5; D. Robertson 5-0; J. Vilma 4-1; J. Glenn 3-0; R. Tongue 3-1; T. Buckley 2-0; S. Ellis 2-4; V. Hobson 2-0
New England R. Harrison 7-3; T. Johnson 6-3; E. Wilson 5-2; T. Bruschi 4-6; J. Green 3-0; T. Law 3-1; R. Seymour 3-2; M. Vrabel 3-1; R. Gay 2-1; A. Samuel 2-0

#54 TEDY BRUSCHI

Want to know why Tedy Bruschi is one of the most popular Patriots players of all time? Want to know why fans line up to get a glimpse of the veteran linebacker? Why he draws the biggest cheers at training camp? Why his No. 54 has been a consistent best-seller in the team's pro shop?

Just listen to him talk about why he signed a contract extension with the Patriots this spring, giving up the opportunity to make a bigger killing as a free agent after the season.

"How much is enough?" Bruschi said following a practice at Gillette Stadium. "How much do you need? I live in North Attleboro. I don't live glamorously. I live in a nice home and we're happy where we are. You really have to look yourself in the eye and say, 'Do you want to go out there and chase every single dime?' Or do you want to stay somewhere and establish something. I chose to stay and establish something."

Bruschi was scheduled to be an unrestricted free agent after the 2004 season. But instead of playing out the year and taking his chances, he "settled" for a four-year, $8.1 million contract with a $3.5 million signing bonus. To be sure, those aren't welfare wages. But when you consider that the franchise number (the average of the top 10 highest paid players at the position) for NFL linebackers is more than $4 million per year, Bruschi certainly didn't break the bank.

Bruschi is considered by many to be a top 10 linebacker, and if he's not, he's definitely close. By anyone's estimation, a deal averaging $2 million a season was on the low end.

Bruschi doesn't employ an agent and handles negotiations himself.

"I'll tell you this," he said. "If I had an agent I wouldn't be here. Agents tell you, 'I can get you more.' But after they say that, it's always, 'But it's going to have to be somewhere else.' And then the player has to make that decision. And I didn't need to make that decision."

Some of Bruschi's teammates were said to be perplexed that he would settle for a below-market deal, thereby strengthening the internal salary cap on the Pats.

"I've only received countless congratulations from my teammates," Bruschi said. "To play out the year and be a free agent, it's a lot of speculation. I don't want to live by 'What ifs?' What if something happens the first month of the season? The AFC Championship Game, when I hurt my calf. Remember? You never know what's going to happen. The Patriots came to me good-heartedly and said, 'Let's get something done to keep you here,' and I said, 'Let's do it.'"

Anyone who saw Bruschi playing on the field with his two young sons, Tedy Jr. and Rex, knows how important family is to him. And in the Pats, he has a good match. The players' wives and children are always around.

"Some things are just more important to me," Bruschi said. "It's been said that if I was a free agent I could have gone out there and made more money, but that's just not important to me. What's important to me is the friendships I have on the team. The fans I've been around for nine years now."

As for the fans, the bond with Bruschi remains incredibly strong.

"I relate to them," he said. "They are my kind of people. Just blue-collar, hard-working people that just work hard and love their families and do the best they can to get the job done. That's the way I would describe the people in the stands—and that's how I would describe myself.

"I'll tell you something that would just kill me," Bruschi added. "To go to another team and then come play a game here and see all those people wearing No. 54 jerseys in the stands. That's something I couldn't take."

—By Michael Felger, *Boston Herald*

Position: *Linebacker*
Height: *6'1"*
Weight: *247*
Born: *6/9/73*
College: *Arizona*
NFL Experience: *9 years*

PATRIOTS HIT STEEL

By Michael Felger, *Boston Herald*

I t was coming. It may not have seemed like it, given how long it had been (399 days to be exact), but it was coming.

The Patriots finally lost a football game after an NFL-record 21 consecutive victories—and it wasn't pretty. The Steelers made the Pats look jittery and mistake-prone in rolling to a 34-20 win, and when it was over the Pats' air of invincibility had been shattered.

Injuries were a factor, to be sure. The Pats entered the game without running back Corey Dillon, and they lost cornerback Ty Law on the third series and left tackle Matt Light in the fourth quarter. They were also without starting corner Tyrone Poole and starting right tackle Tom Ashworth. That left them vulnerable at key spots across the field, and it showed.

But there was something about the way the Pats lost that had to be concerning. The Pats came unglued, committing four turnovers that led to 24 Steelers points. The entire team got beat up. The defense got run over.

So while no one was flipping over chairs in the Pats' locker room afterward, no one was willing to pin the loss on the injuries, either.

ABOVE: Ike Taylor makes an interception, one of four Patriots turnovers in the game.
(Michael Seamans/Boston Herald)

"I've been in this game a long time. I don't make excuses," said linebacker Willie McGinest. "It's a tough pill to swallow. We don't ever say, 'That was a good loss. We needed that.' That's not what we do."

Added Richard Seymour: "We're not going to make any excuses about what happened, why it happened. We just took one on the chin and we have to bounce back from it. That's our attitude."

Bill Belichick was especially stern, grimacing when asked if he could take any positive from the game.

"No, we got beat," Belichick said. "We got killed.

"They outcoached us. They outplayed us. We weren't very good in any phase of the game. We just didn't do anything near the way we're capable of doing it. Pittsburgh played an outstanding game. So that's about the result you would expect when those two forces collide."

There were some truly scary numbers for the Pats. Without Dillon, Kevin Faulk and the running game had minus-one yard through three quarters and five yards on the day. The dismantled offensive line gave up four sacks and countless pressures. The run defense got steamrolled, with Duce Staley and Jerome Bettis contributing to the Steelers' 221-yard day. Quarterback Ben Roethlisberger was allowed to look like the second coming, as he completed 18-of-24 passes with two touchdowns, no interceptions and no sacks.

The worst part may have been the run defense, which contributed to the Steelers having a whopping 42:58-17:02 advantage in time of possession.

"They ran it down our throats, and that's disappointing," safety Rodney Harrison said. "You have to be able to get off the field and at least give your offense a chance. If you can't stop the run, you can't win in this league."

The game turned dramatically over the course of a dozen plays in the first quarter, start-

	1st	2nd	3rd	4th	Final
New England	3	7	3	7	20
Pittsburgh	21	3	10	0	34

Scoring Summary

New England Adam Vinatieri 43-yard field goal. Seven plays, 40 yards in 2:18.
Pittsburgh Plaxico Burress 47-yard pass from Ben Roethlisberger (Reed kick). Six plays, 80 yards in 4:10.
Pittsburgh Plaxico Burress four-yard pass from Ben Roethlisberger (Reed kick). Five plays, 27 yards in 3:02.
Pittsburgh Deshea Townsend 39-yard interception return (Reed kick).
Pittsburgh Jeff Reed 19-yard field goal. Nine plays, 79 yards in 5:29.
New England David Givens two-yard pass from Tom Brady (Vinatieri kick). Seven plays, 56 yards in 1:24.
Pittsburgh Jerome Bettis two-yard run (Reed kick). Four plays, 17 yards in 1:37.
New England Adam Vinatieri 25-yard field goal. Eleven plays, 59 yards in 2:25.
Pittsburgh Jeff Reed 29-yard field goal. Fourteen plays, 61 yards in 8:35.
New England David Givens 23-yard pass from Tom Brady (Vinatieri kick). Ten plays, 86 yards in 3:14.

Team Statistics

Category	New England	Pittsburgh
First Downs	19	25
Rushes-Yards (Net)	6-5	49-221
Passing-Yards (Net)	243	196
Passes Att-Comp-Int	43-25-2	24-18-0
Total Offense Plays-Yards	53-248	73-417
Punt Returns-Yards	3-15	2-10
Kickoff Returns-Yards	6-158	5-136
Punts (Number-Avg)	3-52.3	4-44.2
Fumbles-Lost	3-2	1-0
Penalties-Yards	6-55	9-90
Possession Time	17:02	42:58
Sacks by (Number-Yards)	0-0	4-28

Individual Offensive Statistics

Rushing: **New England** K. Faulk 5-4; C. Cobbs 1-1
Pittsburgh D. Staley 25-125; J. Bettis 15-65; V. Haynes 3-17; H. Ward 1-11; B. Roethlisberger 5-3

Passing: **New England** T. Brady 25-43-2-271
Pittsburgh B. Roethlisberger 18-24-2-196

Receiving: **New England** D. Givens 8-101; K. Faulk 8-72; T. Brown 5-59; D. Patten 4-39
Pittsburgh P. Burress 3-63; H. Ward 6-58; A. Randle El 6-44; V. Haynes 2-18; D. Kreider 1-13

Individual Defensive Statistics

Interceptions: **New England** none
Pittsburgh D. Townsend 1; I. Taylor 1

Sacks: **New England** none
Pittsburgh J. Porter 3; A. Smith 1

Tackles (unassisted-assisted): **New England** R. Harrison 13-8; T. Johnson 6-4; T. Bruschi 5-4; T. Warren 5-0; E. Wilson 5-3; R. Gay 4-0; M. Vrabel 4-3; A. Samuel 3-0; R. Seymour 3-6; V. Wilfork 3-1; R. Colvin 2-1; R. Phifer 2-0; K. Traylor 2-1
Pittsburgh C. Iwuoma 4-0; J. Porter 4-3; W. Williams 4-1; J. Farrior 3-2; T. Polamalu 3-0; R. Colclough 2-0; L. Foote 2-0; C. Haggans 2-0; R. Stuvaints 2-1; D. Townsend 2-1; K. von Oelhoffen 2-1

ABOVE: Rookie sensation Ben Roethlisberger stands in the pocket to deliver a pass as Richard Seymour closes in behind him. *(Michael Seamans/Boston Herald)*

ing when Law left the game after getting beat by Hines Ward on a slant pattern. Two plays later, Plaxico Burress beat rookie free agent Randall Gay for a 47-yard touchdown catch. Brady then gave it right back, fumbling on a strip sack by Joey Porter, setting up another Burress touchdown. On the next snap, Bethel Johnson slipped on his pattern, allowing Deshea Townsend to step in front of a Brady pass and take it back 39 yards for an easy score.

Any chance the Pats had at a comeback was killed when Faulk fumbled on the first play of the second half, setting up another Steelers score.

"It's frustrating," Harrison said. "Eventually, you might lose a game. But you just don't like to lose it in that fashion. But there's no need to push the panic button. It's one game. We have a lot of football left."

ABOVE: Tom Brady hangs his head and paces the sidelines late in the fourth quarter. The Steelers pounded Brady and the Patriots, forcing several costly turnovers. (Michael Seamans/Boston Herald)

PATS JAM RAMS

By George Kimball, *Boston Herald*

As late as Friday, wide receiver Troy Brown was listed as "questionable" on the Patriots' injury report.

Though bothered by a shoulder injury, Brown was in uniform at the Edward Jones Dome, and by time the St. Louis Rams ran their second play from scrimmage, he knew he might be in for a very busy afternoon. Cornerbacks Ty Law and Tyrone Poole hadn't dressed for the game, and on the second play, Asante Samuel didn't get up after a violent collision with Rams tight end Brandon Manumaleuna.

The Patriots were missing their top three cornerbacks.

"Tell me about it," coach Bill Belichick said.

As he saw Samuel down on the turf, Brown suspected his number was about to come up.

Brown wouldn't hazard a guess as to how many of the game's 114 plays he participated in, but for the rest of the afternoon he was the third receiver and the fifth defensive back for a team that frequently employed both formations in its 40-22 victory.

"I have no idea," Brown said. "I'd be in trouble if I started counting them."

ABOVE: Tedy Bruschi takes down quarterback Marc Bulger for a sack in the second half.
(Michael Seamans/Boston Herald)

ABOVE: Kicker Adam Vinatieri throws a four-yard touchdown pass to Troy Brown in the third quarter.
(Michael Seamans/Boston Herald)

Brown's line: Three catches for 30 yards (including a sneak-attack pass for a touchdown from kicker Adam Vinatieri), three tackles, a pass defended and a pass interference penalty.

"Troy had got some work there in preseason," Belichick said of his decision to employ Brown on defense. "He had some experience, and he stepped in and played well."

Brown said he was prepared to step up.

"We've had some unfortunate things happen to our DBs so far. We got one short-handed today," Brown said. "You never know in this game, and it's like the guy [Samuel] got hurt pretty quick. Those things happen, so you've got to be ready at all times. I prepared myself for the situation and it worked out in my favor."

Brown said he embraced Belichick's suggestion that he work out with the defensive backs last summer.

"Man, I welcomed it with open arms," Brown said. "I'm a football player, and any chance I have to get on the field, I want to be out there. But I didn't want to be out there just taking up space. I wanted to go out there and play well."

	1st	2nd	3rd	4th	Final
New England	6	13	14	7	40
St. Louis	0	14	0	8	22

Scoring Summary

New England Adam Vinatieri 43-yard field goal. Seven plays, 47 yards in 3:35.
New England Adam Vinatieri 31-yard field goal. Five plays, 15 yards in 1:49.
St. Louis Leonard Little zero-yard fumble return (Wilkins kick).
New England Mike Vrabel two-yard pass from Tom Brady (Vinatieri kick). Ten plays, 64 yards in 5:42.
St. Louis Isaac Bruce 11-yard pass from Marc Bulger (Wilkins kick). Six plays, 85 yards in 3:45.
New England Adam Vinatieri 45-yard field goal. Five plays, 46 yards in 2:16.
New England Adam Vinatieri 36-yard field goal. Nine plays, 54 yards in 1:02.
New England Troy Brown four-yard pass from Adam Vinatieri (Vinatieri kick). Nine plays, 54 yards in 4:34.
New England Corey Dillon five-yard run (Vinatieri kick). Four plays, 21 yards in 2:07.
St. Louis Torry Holt 16-yard pass from Marc Bulger (Faulk run). Eleven plays, 73 yards in 4:23.
New England Bethel Johnson four-yard pass from Tom Brady (Vinatieri kick). Nine plays, 64 yards in 5:29.

Team Statistics

Category	New England	St. Louis
First Downs	22	21
Rushes-Yards (Net)	32-147	19-81
Passing-Yards (Net)	229	259
Passes Att-Comp-Int	32-19-0	33-23-1
Total Offense Plays-Yards	66-376	57-340
Punt Returns-Yards	2-22	2-3
Kickoff Returns-Yards	4-85	7-159
Punts (Number-Avg)	2-45.5	4-42.5
Fumbles-Lost	1-1	2-2
Penalties-Yards	6-48	9-80
Possession Time	31:45	28:15
Sacks by (Number-Yards)	5-26	2-9

Individual Offensive Statistics

Rushing: **New England** C. Dillon 25-112; P. Pass 3-25; K. Faulk 1-9; T. Brady 3-1
St. Louis M. Faulk 12-66; M. Bulger 2-14; S. Jackson 3-1; S. McDonald 2-0

Passing: **New England** T. Brady 18-31-2-234; A. Vinatieri 1-1-1-4
St. Louis M. Bulger 23-33-2-285

Receiving: **New England** D. Givens 5-100; D. Patten 2-34; P. Pass 3-32; T. Brown 3-30; C. Dillon 2-19; K. Faulk 2-17; B. Johnson 1-4; M. Vrabel 1-2
St. Louis T. Holt 6-111; I. Bruce 4-59; B. Manumaleuna 3-53; S. McDonald 3-33; M. Faulk 6-22; K. Curtis 1-7

Individual Defensive Statistics

Interceptions: **New England** R. Phifer 1
St. Louis none

Sacks : **New England** T. Bruschi 1; W. McGinest 1; R. Seymour 1; T. Warren 1; J. Green 1
St. Louis D. Lewis 1; T. Jackson 1

Tackles (unassisted-assisted): **New England** R. Harrison 8-0; M. Vrabel 5-0; E. Wilson 5-0; T. Brown 3-0; L. Izzo 3-0; D. Reid 3-0; K. Traylor 3-0; T. Bruschi 2-1; D. Davis 2-0; T. Johnson 2-0; W. McGinest 2-0; R. Seymour 2-0; T. Warren 2-0
St. Louis A. Archuleta 6-0; J. Butler 6-0; D. Lewis 6-1; T. Faulk 5-1; T. Polley 4-2; R. Coady 3-0; T. Jackson 3-0; J. Kennedy 3-0; L. Little 3-0; P. Tinoisamoa 3-2; T. Fisher 2-1; E. Flowers 2-0; D. Groce 2-0; R. Pickett 2-0; J. Wilkins 2-0

PATS POUND BLEDSOE

By Michael Felger, *Boston Herald*

I t's hard to tell whether the Patriots are really as good they looked, or whether Drew Bledsoe is just that bad.

The Pats once again embarrassed Bledsoe at Gillette Stadium, rolling to their 23rd victory in 24 games with a 29-6 romp over the Bills.

The night began with an appearance by Red Sox ownership, players Curt Schilling and Johnny Damon and the Sox' World Series trophy.

The display showed that some things in sports do change.

Then Bledsoe came on the field and proved that other things change. Bill Belichick is still Bledsoe's daddy.

"Drew's a good friend of mine and I love the guy to death. But football can be bittersweet and crappy," said kicker Adam Vinatieri, sounding a note of pity that permeated the Patriots' locker room. "We tried to make it hard on him the best we could. Bill finds a way to throw a wrinkle every time that puts a little pressure on him."

ABOVE: Bills quarterback Drew Bledsoe is sacked by Tully Banta-Cain to end the second quarter.
(Matthew West/Boston Herald)

BELOW: Bethel Johnson pulls in a 47-yard catch for the first down. *(Nancy Lane/Boston Herald)*

Thanks to that pressure, Bledsoe completed just eight-of-19 passes for 76 yards with no touchdowns, three interceptions and a ludicrous quarterback rating of 14.3.

The ultimate indignity came early in the fourth quarter, when receiver Troy Brown, playing as a slot corner, intercepted a wayward Bledsoe pass and returned it 17 yards. In three career games at Gillette as a member of the Bills, Bledsoe has thrown eight interceptions and taken seven sacks.

"There's not much really to say after tonight," Bledsoe said.

Added Brown: "That's my boy. So it's tough to watch. I love him to death, and I wish him the best of luck. ...But in a competitive spirit, I've got to do what I've got to do."

The Pats also stuffed the resurgent running game of the Bills, holding them to 50 yards as a team. Willis McGahee gained just 37 yards on 14 carries.

Meanwhile, the Patriots beat the Bills at their own game, grinding out 208 yards on the ground, 151 of which came from plow horse Corey Dillon. The Bills had not allowed a 100-yard rushing game all season, but Dillon blew that stat out of the water.

"When you get 100 on those guys, it's well-deserved," Dillon said.

Meanwhile, Tom Brady was off-target on many throws, but he hit a few big ones that counted the most, including touchdown passes of 13 yards to David Patten and five yards to Christian Fauria in the second quarter.

The red zone was a problem again for the offense, as the Pats had to settle for five Vinatieri field goals. But those issues were never really a factor because the outcome was never in doubt.

For the 17th consecutive game, the Pats scored first (on a 27-yard Vinatieri chip shot) and Brady's two scoring strikes made it 20-0 at the half.

	1st	2nd	3rd	4th	Final
Buffalo	0	0	6	0	6
New England	3	17	3	6	29

Scoring Summary

New England Adam Vinatieri 27-yard field goal. Twelve plays, 81 yards in 5:58.
New England Adam Vinatieri 24-yard field goal. Eleven plays, 91 yards in 4:33.
New England David Patten 13-yard pass from Tom Brady (Vinatieri kick). Eleven plays, 75 yards in 5:29.
New England Christian Fauria five-yard pass from Tom Brady (Vinatieri kick). Four plays, 27 yards in 1:35.
New England Adam Vinatieri 20-yard field goal. Thirteen plays, 70 yards in 5:52.
Buffalo Jonathan Smith 70-yard punt return (McGahee run failed).
New England Adam Vinatieri 45-yard field goal. Six plays, 49 yards in 2:38.
New England Adam Vinatieri 37-yard field goal. Twelve plays, 50 yards in 6:54.

Team Statistics

Category	Buffalo	New England
First Downs	8	25
Rushes-Yards (Net)	17-50	45-208
Passing-Yards (Net)	75	220
Passes Att-Comp-Int	21-9-4	35-19-1
Total Offense Plays-Yards	41-125	82-428
Punt Returns-Yards	2-70	3-34
Kickoff Returns-Yards	7-142	2-48
Punts (Number-Avg)	5-48.0	3-46.7
Fumbles-Lost	1-1	1-0
Penalties-Yards	2-48	5-44
Possession Time	18:38	41:22
Sacks by (Number-Yards)	2-13	3-6

Individual Offensive Statistics

Rushing: **Buffalo** W. McGahee 14-37; D. Bledsoe 1-8; J. Losman 1-5; J. Burns 1-0.
New England C. Dillon 26-151; K. Faulk 13-61; T. Brady 1-2; R. Davey 1-minus 1; R. Abdullah 4-minus 5.

Passing: **Buffalo** D. Bledsoe 8-19-0-76; J. Losman 1-2-0-5
New England T. Brady 19-35-2-233.

Receiving: **Buffalo** E. Moulds 5-46; L. Evans 1-15; W. McGahee 1-12; D. Shelton 1-5; T. Euhus 1-3.
New England D. Givens 5-66; B. Johnson 1-47; D. Patten 3-43; T. Brown 2-23; K. Faulk 2-16; J. Weaver 1-10; D. Graham 1-9; P. Pass 2-9; C. Dillon 1-5; C. Fauria 1-5.

Individual Defensive Statistics

Interceptions: **Buffalo** N. Clements 1.
New England T. Banta-Cain 1; T. Bruschi 1; E. Wilson 1; T. Brown 1.

Sacks: **Buffalo** S. Adams 1; C. Kelsay 1.
New England T. Banta-Cain 1.5; W. McGinest 1; R. Colvin .5.

Tackles (unassisted-assisted): **Buffalo** L. Milloy 10-5; L. Fletcher 7-4; T. Spikes 6-5; J. Posey 5-3; S. Adams 4-1; R. Baker 4-0; A. Schobel 4-4; P. Williams 4-2; J. Greer 3-0; T. McGee 3-0; N. Clements 2-1; C. Kelsay 2-1; E. Moulds 2-0; I. Reese 2-2.
New England R. Gay 4-0; T. Johnson 4-0; M. Vrabel 4-2; T. Banta-Cain 3-3; T. Bruschi 3-3; W. McGinest 3-1; J. Cherry 2-0; E. Moreland 2-0; T. Warren 2-3.

ABOVE: Patriots Troy Brown (80), Roman Phifer, and Randall Gay (21) celebrate Brown's fourth-quarter interception. The Pats' defense intercepted Bledsoe three times in the game. *(Matthew West/Boston Herald)*

The Bills' lone dent on the scoreboard came on Jonathan Smith's 70-yard punt return for a touchdown in the third quarter.

"Overall, I thought it was a pretty solid effort," Belichick said. "You shut a team out on defense, you have to feel pretty good about that."

ABOVE: Tom Brady throws a pass in the fourth quarter. Brady finished the night with 19 completions and 233 yards. *(Matthew West/Boston Herald)*

Arrowhead Stadium

PATS KEEP ROLLING

By Michael Felger, *Boston Herald*

They've gone into the toughest environments, played the most high-powered offenses and suffered injuries at the most important positions. And still the Patriots keep winning.

If that surprises you, like it seems to surprise many national observers, then the Pats have a message for you: Get used to it. After surviving yet another offensive juggernaut in hostile territory, beating the Chiefs, 27-19, the players in the visitors locker room at Arrowhead Stadium seemed to have no patience for the incessant question: How do you keep doing it?

"When are you going to realize we've got playmakers on this defense?" snapped linebacker Tedy Bruschi. "Everyone keeps asking me how we do it. How do we do it? We've got good players! Does this surprise me? Absolutely not."

Bruschi's pride notwithstanding, the Pats don't currently have the greatest players in their banged-up secondary (hello, Earthwind Moreland). That's why they gave up their share of plays up and down the field.

ABOVE: **Troy Brown shakes Greg Wesley loose for a long gain in the second quarter.**
(Michael Seamans/Boston Herald)

ABOVE: Rodney Harrison and Asante Samuel attempt to break up a Chiefs pass in the third quarter.
(Michael Seamans/Boston Herald)

But, true to form, the Pats made the crucial plays when they had to, and the biggest of all were Rodney Harrison's end zone interception late in the first half and Willie McGinest's game-ending sack with the Chiefs driving for the potential tying score.

Offensively, the Pats never had to play catch-up, and that led to some good balance between Tom Brady and Corey Dillon. The offense also got a huge boost from the return of top receiver Deion Branch.

The game did have some anxious moments, none more nerve-racking than Dillon's fumble on the Chiefs' three-yard line with 12:04 remaining and the Pats leading by 11. A touchdown would have given the Pats an insurmountable lead. Instead, the turnover set up a 26-yard touchdown pass from Trent Green to Eddie Kennison, who was all alone in the end zone after Moreland's second touchdown-producing mistake of the game.

The Chiefs failed on their two-point attempt, which meant the Pats had to run some clock or produce a score to seal the win. They did both, as Dillon held onto the ball while running for 28 yards and Adam Vinatieri made it an eight-point cushion with a 28-yard field goal.

On the ensuing possession, McGinest dropped Green for a sack on fourth down and the Pats had their third straight win.

"It's a tough place to come in and play," said coach Bill Belichick. "I thought the players did a good job standing up to the adversity."

Surprised?

	1st	2nd	3rd	4th	Final
New England	7	10	7	3	27
Kansas City	10	0	3	6	19

Scoring Summary

New England Corey Dillon five-yard run (Vinatieri kick). Ten plays, 71 yards in 4:31.

Kansas City Lawrence Tynes 44-yard field goal. Five plays, 30 yards in 2:42.

Kansas City Eddie Kennison 65-yard pass from Trent Green (Tynes kick. Five plays, 84 yards in 2:34.

New England Corey Dillon one-yard run (Vinatieri kick. Ten plays, 75 yards in 4:35.

New England Adam Vinatieri 37-yard field goal. Six plays, 37 yards in 2:19.

Kansas City Lawrence Tynes 24-yard field goal. Fifteen plays, 68 yards in 8:15.

New England Deion Branch 26-yard pass from Tom Brady (Vinatieri kick. Four plays, 75 yards in 1:51.

Kansas City Eddie Kennison 26-yard pass from Trent Green (Kennison pass from Green failed). Eleven plays, 97 yards in 5:45.

New England Adam Vinatieri 28-yard field goal. Eleven plays, 54 yards in 4:27.

Team Statistics

Category	New England	Kansas City
First Downs	21	20
Rushes-Yards (Net)	32-98	20-64
Passing-Yards (Net)	309	353
Passes Att-Comp-Int	26-17-0	42-27-1
Total Offense Plays-Yards	59-407	66-417
Punt Returns-Yards	1-4	1-0
Kickoff Returns-Yards	5-94	6-156
Punts (Number-Avg)	2-43.5	3-31.7
Fumbles-Lost	1-1	1-0
Penalties-Yards	4-25	7-50
Possession Time	27:59	32:01
Sacks by (Number-Yards)	4-28	1-6

Individual Offensive Statistics

Rushing: **New England** C. Dillon 26-98; K. Faulk 1-1; T. Brady 5-minus 1
Kansas City D. Blaylock 19-58; T. Green 1-6

Passing: **New England** T. Brady 17-26-1-315
Kansas City T. Green 27-42-2-381

Receiving: **New England** D. Branch 6-105; D. Graham 3-83; D. Patten 1-46; T. Brown 2-27; C. Dillon 1-20; P. Pass 2-17; C. Fauria 1-14; D. Givens 1-3
Kansas City J. Morton 5-107; E. Kennison 3-99; T. Gonzalez 7-86; D. Blaylock 5-33; D. Hall 3-32; J. Dunn 3-17; T. Richardson 1-7

Individual Defensive Statistics

Interceptions: **New England** R. Harrison 1
Kansas City none

Sacks: **New England** T. Warren 2; W. McGinest 1; R. Colvin 1
Kansas City J. Allen 1

Tackles (unassisted-assisted): **New England** R. Harrison 8-0; T. Bruschi 7-0; T. Warren 7-0; M. Vrabel 5-1; A. Samuel 4-0; W. McGinest 3-0; D. Reid 3-0; E. Wilson 3-0; R. Gay 2-0; T. Johnson 2-0; K. Traylor 2-1; V. Wilfork 2-0
Kansas City K. Mitchell 8-0; G. Wesley 5-2; J. Allen 4-0; Q. Caver 4-0; E. Warfield 4-0; J. Battle 3-0; B. Sapp 3-0; J. Woods 3-1; J. Browning 2-1; L. Dalton 2-0; S. Harts 2-

PATRIOTS ADAPT, WIN

By Michael Gee, *Boston Herald*

Some Americans reject the theory of evolution. The Patriots embrace it. New England reproduces victories like mad by adapting to their environment better than any species in the NFL. They're Charles Darwin's team.

Does an opponent want to trade fireworks displays in a game full of long passes and end-to-end offensive rushes? The Pats will happily set off more Roman candles than the other guys, as they did to beat the Chiefs in Kansas City.

On the other hand, some opponents live off defense, special teams, and error avoidance, like the Baltimore Ravens. Some NFL games are played in weather so bad first downs become minor miracles.

The Pats seamlessly adapted to both circumstances, kicking the sodden Ravens around the swamp of Gillette Stadium for a 24-3 victory. Shootout or hog-wallow, the Patriots adjust their way to the left side of the final score.

In less than a week, the Pats outscored pro football's top offense in an aerial circus, then switched gears and thrashed the NFL's top defensive team. That's the most basic reason New England's 10-1 this year, why it's won 25

ABOVE: Ravens receiver Travis Taylor is swarmed by Patriots Ted Johnson, Rodney Harrison and Eugene Wilson. *(Matthew West/Boston Herald)*

BELOW: Corey Dillon drags Terrell Suggs for extra yards in the first quarter. Dillon rushed for 130 yards against the Ravens. *(Stuart Cahill/Boston Herald)*

of its last 26 games. The Pats let the other guys call the tune, then never miss a note.

"That's football," said Pats safety Rodney Harrison. "It's all about adjustments. Sometimes you're in a shootout like we were against Indy or KC. Sometimes you're in a slugfest like this one. You have to have the ability to adapt to different styles of football."

The Pats don't merely adjust to styles. They make them their own. Imagine if Robert DeNiro was cast in a big-budget movie based on your life. He'd be a better you than you are. That's what the Ravens went through. The Pats gave a faultless rendition of Baltimore's game plan. They out-Ravened 'em.

To win, the Ravens want to stop the other team's running game, force its quarterback into mistakes and capitalize on turnovers. They've scored as many TDs on returns as on passes this season. Baltimore is undefeated when it intercepts a pass, winless when it can't. Mr. Belichick, could you have your team give that script a run-through?

Corey Dillon ran 30 times for 123 yards, mostly wide away from Ray Lewis and onto dry ground. Tom Brady completed 15-of-30 passes for only 172 yards, but didn't throw an interception. Brady averaged 12.1 yards a throw in Kansas City, and less than half that against the Ravens. Each performance was the perfect thing to do.

In frightful weather, the lead is of transcendant importance, and it's usually provided by one's place kicker. Adam Vinatieri went three-for-three on field goals to give the Pats a 9-3 lead after three periods. Vinatieri adores winter gales. He probably bicycled to work—in shorts.

On defense, the Pats held the Ravens to 2.1 yards a play. Without Jamal Lewis, Baltimore couldn't run, so Kyle Boller couldn't pass. He was 15-of-35 for 93 yards, was sacked six times and threw an interception. Rubbing it in, the Pats concluded their scoring with, what else, a defensive touchdown. Tedy Bruschi forced a

	1st	2nd	3rd	4th	Final
Baltimore	0	3	0	0	3
New England	0	3	6	15	24

Scoring Summary
New England Adam Vinatieri 28-yard field goal. Thirteen plays, 59 yards in 5:57.
Baltimore Matt Stover 22-yard field goal. Six plays, 12 yards in 0:34.
New England Adam Vinatieri 40-yard field goal. Nine plays, 37 yards in 3:38.
New England Adam Vinatieri 48-yard field goal. Six plays, 22 yards in 3:32.
New England Corey Dillon one-yard run (Dillon run). Nine plays, 48 yards in 4:41.
New England Jarvis Green zero-yard fumble return (Vinatieri kick).

Team Statistics
Category	Baltimore	New England
First Downs	8	18
Rushes-Yards (Net)	20-77	41-144
Passing-Yards (Net)	47	170
Passes Att-Comp-Int	35-15-1	30-15-0
Total Offense Plays-Yards	59-124	72-314
Punt Returns-Yards	3-32	6-38
Kickoff Returns-Yards	6-106	2-45
Punts (Number-Avg)	10-44.4	8-32.1
Fumbles-Lost	2-1	3-0
Penalties-Yards	10-106	10-97
Possession Time	24:06	35:54
Sacks by (Number-Yards)	1-2	4-46

Individual Offensive Statistics
Rushing: **Baltimore** C. Taylor 16-61; K. Boller 2-10; J. White 2-6
New England C. Dillon 30-123; P. Pass 4-12; K. Faulk 3-7; T. Brady 3-3; R. Davey 1-minus 1

Passing: **Baltimore** K. Boller 15-35-0-93
New England T. Brady 15-30-0-172

Receiving: **Baltimore** D. Wilcox 2-30; C. Taylor 5-24; K. Johnson 3-20; C. Moore 2-15; T. Taylor 1-4; R. Hymes 1-0; A. Ricard 1-0
New England D. Branch 4-51; D. Givens 6-42; D. Patten 1-37; D. Graham 2-24; P. Pass 2-18

Individual Defensive Statistics
Interceptions: **Baltimore** none
New England R. Gay 1

Sacks): **Baltimore** M. Douglas 1
New England T. Johnson 1; T. Bruschi 1; R. Colvin 1; R. Seymour 1

Tackles (unassisted-assisted): **Baltimore** R. Lewis 8-4; E. Reed 7-2; W. Demps 6-3; A. Thomas 5-1; G. Baxter 4-1; T. Suggs 4-0; T. Weaver 4-1; M. Douglas 3-2; R. Walls 3-1; C. Fuller 2-1; K. Gregg 2-3; J. Johnson 2-2; M. Kemoeatu 2-0; C. Williams 2-3
New England R. Harrison 9-4; T. Johnson 6-3; T. Bruschi 4-3; E. Wilson 4-0; R. Colvin 3-0; L. Izzo 3-0; D. Davis 2-4; R. Gay 2-0; E. Moreland 2-1; P. Pass 2-0; V. Wilfork 2-1

ABOVE: Richard Seymour takes down beleagured Ravens quarterback Kyle Boller. Boller was sacked six times and threw one interception. *(Stuart Cahill/Boston Herald)*

Boller fumble, which Jarvis Green recovered in the end zone.

The Patriots, in short, were the Ravens of Brian Billick's dreams. In conditions that insured an imperfect game, New England played imperfect football better than the other chaps.

The Pats will change anything in a football game but its outcome.

ABOVE: Tom Brady charges through the line on a quarterback keeper in the first quarter.
(Stuart Cahill/Boston Herald)

#4 ADAM VINATIERI

The guessing here is that Adam Vinatieri crawled out of bed Sunday morning and took a look out the window, after which the man addressed his trusty right foot and said, "Lil' fella, you're gonna be busy today."

It's a gridiron thing. When the weather outside is frightful, the kicking can be so delightful.

When the weather gets bad—and I mean REAL bad—you've got these brawny, overstuffed running backs turning into Hanna Barbera characters as they try to tote the ball, their legs going a mile a minute but their bodies, and hence, the ball, going nowhere. As for the quarterbacks, a typical play has them throwing crisp passes to an invisible receiver at the 18, this because the receiver, as well as the cornerback covering him, have slipped in the mud back at the 30.

The kicker, then, essentially becomes the star quarterback. And so it was at Gillette Stadium Sunday, as Vinatieri, acting as though the rain and the mud made for perfect football weather, kicked three field goals in the Patriots' 24-3 victory over the Baltimore Ravens.

So tell us, Adam, when you looked out the window Sunday morning and saw those clouds, what crossed your mind?

"Wear long spikes on your shoes and hope for the best," he said.

And for a good chunk of the day, it appeared the only scoring would be provided by the men who think with their feet. The Pats led 9-3 going into the fourth quarter, with Vinatieri providing field goals of 28, 40 and 48 yards, and the Ravens' Matt Stover chipping in with a 22-yarder.

The Pats then padded their lead when Corey Dillon scored on a one-yard touchdown run, after which Dillon provided a two-point conversion. Later, Tedy Bruschi forced a fumble by Baltimore quarterback Kyle Boller, with Jarvis Green picking up the loose ball in the end zone.

Those are the kind of plays—balls bouncing on the field, players sliding around, the likes of Green scoring touchdowns—that you get on days like that. Yet you never

see Vinatieri swept away by the wind, drowned by the raindrops, buried in the snow.

The guy just kicks the ball. Memo to David Letterman: Forget the bit where Vinatieri kicks balls off of Manhattan rooftops. Instead, wait till it snows and then get him down there on that street next to the Ed Sullivan Theater and watch him do his thing.

"Those long field goals, had they been at the other end of the field, I'm not so sure we would even have attempted them," Pats coach Bill Belichick said after Sunday's game. "There was a little footing out there at the lighthouse end, but he did a great job of kicking them. He got the ball up, and they were true, and they were tough conditions."

Then Belichick provided, if you'll pardon the expression, the kicker: "There's no kicker I'd rather have. Let's put it that way."

Understand that Vinatieri is yet another Patriot who has signed on with that Team Concept thing, which sounds about as corny as August in Kansas. But that corny Team Concept thing has earned the Pats two Super Bowl trophies over the last three years.

Asked if he is, you know, just made for bad weather, given what he did Sunday and especially what he did against Oakland in The Snow Game at the late, great Foxboro Stadium, he chose cornball over football.

"I don't want to say that," he said. "There are a lot of good kickers out there. And if it's a home game like this, our fellas are kind of accustomed to playing on a crappy field, and in crappy weather—rain or snow. The bottom line is that it's 11 guys versus 11 guys and the guys who go out and execute and make the best plays are going to win."

Whatever. I just know that, on a bad day, with lots of mud, lots of rain, lots of snow, lots of Shelby Scott coming out of retirement to give us live reports from the WBZ Storm Center, I want Adam Vinatieri loosening up on the sideline.

—By Steve Buckley, *Boston Herald*

Matthew West/Boston Herald

Position: *Kicker*
Height: *6'0"*
Weight: *202*
Born: *12/28/72*
College: *South Dakota State*
NFL Experience: *9 years*

BROWNS, BLACK & BLUE

By Michael Felger, *Boston Herald*

It only felt like a preseason game. Everything else about where the Patriots are is very, very real.

All last week, Bill Belichick spoke about how dangerous Cleveland could be given its midseason coaching change from Butch Davis to Terry Robiskie. That danger was addressed in the first 14 seconds of the game—when Bethel Johnson returned the opening kickoff 93 yards for a touchdown—and from there the Pats rolled. When it was over, most of the starters had gotten a nice rest and the Pats had a 42-15 blowout victory.

The last time the Pats came to Cleveland was 2000, when Drew Bledsoe was still the quarterback and Belichick's old team was limping to a 5-11 season. At the end of the Browns' 19-11 win that day, Belichick was treated to taunts and curses from the sellout crowd, a crude reminder of the five dark years he spent as head coach of the (former) Browns from 1991-95.

Nine years later, Belichick leads one of the top organizations in all of pro sports, while the Browns have organization. But when asked if

ABOVE: **The Patriots congratulate Bethel Johnson (81) after he returned the opening kickoff for a 93-yard**

BELOW: Defensive end Ty Warren shuts down William Green in the first quarter. The Patriots held the Browns to only 46 rushing yards. *(Michael Seamans/Boston Herald)*

yesterday's win was special for him, Belichick was typically deadpan.

"I thought we played better today," he said. Belichick's players were more forthcoming.

"It would mean a lot to me if I were him, let's put it that way," linebacker Tedy Bruschi said. "Especially with the way we lost here the last time. I'm one of the few guys who is still on the team from that. I didn't feel too good about that one, and I'm sure [Belichick] didn't either. That's why I'm happy for him now."

The game was over as soon as it began, as Johnson shook off his season-long struggles and took it to the house on the opening play. Corey Dillon followed up with two short touchdown runs to make it 21-0 in the second quarter. And when Randall Gay picked up a William Green fumble (forced by Seymour) early in the third quarter and returned it 41 yards for another score, the Pats led 28-7 and garbage time was officially on.

The Pats controlled every facet of play during the meaningful moments of the game, particularly early. In the first quarter, the Pats dominated in yards, first downs and time of possession. The Pats finished with season highs in rushing attempts and yards.

On defense, Rodney Harrison made the play of the game with a one-handed interception in the first half. Browns rookie quarterback Luke McCown was mostly overwhelmed.

The Pats aired out their bench in the second half, giving fans a chance to see rookie running back Cedric Cobbs and backup quarterback Rohan Davey in their most extended playing time of the season. Of course, the Pats were able to do that because they jumped on the Browns early.

Said Johnson: "Emotionally, they were looking for life. We didn't want to be a part of that."

	1st	2nd	3rd	4th	Final
New England	14	7	21	0	42
Cleveland	0	7	0	8	15

Scoring Summary

New England Bethel Johnson 93-yard kick return (Vinatieri kick).
New England Corey Dillon four-yard run (Vinatieri kick). Twelve plays, 95 yards in 6:38.
New England Corey Dillon one-yard run (Vinatieri kick). Ten plays, 72 yards in 3:49.
Cleveland Antonio Bryant 16-yard pass from Luke McCown (Dawson kick). Eleven plays, 70 yards in 1:17.
New England Randall Gay 41-yard fumble return (Vinatieri kick).
New England Kevin Faulk 10-yard run (Vinatieri kick). Nine plays, 73 yards in 4:53.
New England David Patten 44-yard pass from Tom Brady (Vinatieri kick). Four plays, 32 yards in 1:15.
Cleveland Antonio Bryant 40-yard pass from Luke McCown (Heiden pass from McCown). Two plays, 93 yards in 0:28.

Team Statistics

Category	New England	Cleveland
First Downs	27	15
Rushes-Yards (Net)	50-225	17-46
Passing-Yards (Net)	187	241
Passes Att-Comp-Int	26-14-1	35-20-2
Total Offense Plays-Yards	78-412	55-287
Punt Returns-Yards	3-5	1-12
Kickoff Returns-Yards	3-134	6-137
Punts (Number-Avg)	3-33.7	4-36.8
Fumbles-Lost	4-2	2-2
Penalties-Yards	8-60	5-84
Possession Time	39:08	20:52
Sacks by (Number-Yards)	3-36	2-14

Individual Offensive Statistics

Rushing: **New England** C. Dillon 18-100; K. Faulk 13-87; C. Cobbs 16-29; T. Brady 1-10; P. Pass 1-1; R. Davey 1-minus 2. **Cleveland** W. Green 12-15; A. Echemandu 3-12; L. McCown 1-11; D. Northcutt 1-8

Passing: **New England** T. Brady 11-20-1-157; R. Davey 3-6-0-44. **Cleveland** L. McCown 20-34-2-277; F. Jackson 0-1-0-0

Receiving: **New England** D. Patten 3-74; C. Fauria 1-25; D. Givens 3-25; B. Johnson 1-20; P. Pass 2-19; D. Graham 1-14; D. Branch 1-13; J. Weaver 1-7; K. Faulk 1-4. **Cleveland** A. Bryant 7-115; D. Northcutt 5-93; A. Echemandu 3-25; W. Green 3-24; S. Heiden 2-20

Individual Defensive Statistics

Interceptions: **New England** T. Brown 1; R. Harrison 1. **Cleveland** L. Sanders 1

Sacks: **New England** T. Bruschi 1; W. McGinest 1; M. Vrabel 1. **Cleveland** K. Lang 2

Tackles (unassisted-assisted): **New England** T. Bruschi 4-1; W. McGinest 4-0; R. Seymour 4-0; T. Brown 3-0; D. Davis 3-0; R. Harrison 3-1; D. Reid 3-1; M. Vrabel 3-1; T. Warren 3-0; T. Banta-Cain 2-0; E. Moreland 2-0; V. Wilfork 2-0; E. Wilson 2-0. **Cleveland** R. Griffith 8-3; L. Sanders 7-0; C. Crocker 6-1; W. Holdman 6-1; K. Lang 6-0; K. Bentley 5-1; B. Gardner 3-4; A. McKinley 3-1; E. Westmoreland 3-0; A. Henry 2-1; E. Little 2-0; M. Myers 2-3; D. Northcutt 2-0; T. Rogers 2-0; O. Roye 2-2; C. Thompson 2-0

PATRIOTS CLINCH

By Michael Felger, *Boston Herald*

The Patriots steamroller has yet to meet an obstacle it can't obliterate. Job-hunting coordinators. (Allegedly) vengeful running backs. Perturbed head coaches. Those items were just more fodder for the Pats' machine.

The Pats clinched the AFC East title and a playoff berth after posting a 35-28 victory over the Cincinnati Bengals at Gillette Stadium. But even though the win raised the Pats' record to a gaudy 12-1 and gave them 27 victories in their last 28 games, there weren't many smiles in the postgame locker room.

Perhaps it had something to do with the distraction involving offensive coordinator Charlie Weis, who will be named the head coach at Notre Dame. Perhaps it had something to do with some uncharacteristically shoddy work on special teams. Surely, it had plenty to do with a defensive effort that allowed the improving Bengals to move the ball at will for much of the game.

Whatever it was, it left Pats coach Bill Belichick clearly agitated.

ABOVE: Asante Samuel returns an interception for a touchdown in the second quarter. The pass from Carson Palmer was intended for Bengals wide receiver T.J. Houshmandzadeh. *(Matthew West/Boston Herald)*

ABOVE: Troy Brown goes airborne to intercept a John Kitna pass in the fourth quarter.
(Nancy Lane/Boston Herald)

"I'd like us to be at our best—that's all," Belichick said. "And I don't think we were today."

It's hard to argue the point, as the Pats allowed 478 yards of total offense and 26 first downs to Carson Palmer, Rudi Johnson and the talented Bengals receiving corps. The game very likely would have been a loss for the Pats had it not been for three ultra-crucial Bengals turnovers—the first (a Johnson fumble) coming at the Pats' 12-yard line, the second (an Asante Samuel interception) being returned for a touchdown, and the third (a Troy Brown interception of Jon Kitna, who replaced an injured Palmer) coming in the end zone.

Those three plays represented a 21-point swing. The Pats won by seven. Do the math.

"I certainly didn't think it was our best game," Belichick said. "We're happy to win, [but] we were fortunate to overcome some of the errors."

The special teams also came up noticeably short, falling asleep on a fake field goal in the third quarter that resulted in an 11-yard touchdown run by holder/punter Kyle Larson and failing to pick up a first down on a quarterback sneak attempt out of a punt formation by Larry Izzo in the fourth quarter.

The Pats were bailed out by Tom Brady, who returned to his old form after two straight mediocre games. Brady was sharp from the outset, completing nine-of-12 passes in the first half and finishing with 260 yards and two touchdowns on 18-of-26 passing. The first touchdown pass was a beautiful, 48-yard deep post to receiver David Patten and the second a 17-yard seam pass to tight end Christian Fauria.

As bad as the Pats' defense was, the Bengals' was worse. Cincinnati couldn't even stop Brady from his backside. A seven-yard completion to back Patrick Pass in the third quarter came while Brady was sitting on the ground.

	1st	2nd	3rd	4th	Final
Cincinnati	0	14	7	7	28
New England	7	21	7	0	35

Scoring Summary

New England Corey Dillon one-yard run (Vinatieri kick). Thirteen plays, 84 yards in 6:18.
Cincinnati Matt Schobel two-yard pass from Carson Palmer (Graham kick). Eleven plays, 45 yards in 5:46.
New England David Patten 48-yard pass from Tom Brady (Vinatieri kick). Three plays, 70 yards in 1:32.
New England Asante Samuel 34-yard interception return (Vinatieri kick).
Cincinnati Chad Johnson five-yard pass from Carson Palmer (Graham kick). Ten plays, 69 yards in 5:48.
New England Kevin Faulk four-yard run (Vinatieri kick). Six plays, 53 yards in 2:09.
New England Christian Fauria 17-yard pass from Tom Brady (Vinatieri kick). Eleven plays, 75 yards in 5:46.
Cincinnati Kyle Larson 11-yard run (Graham kick). Twelve plays, 77 yards in 6:04.
Cincinnati Kelley Washington 27-yard pass from Jon Kitna (Graham kick). Five plays, 61 yards in 2:47.

Team Statistics

Category	Cincinnati	New England
First Downs	26	22
Rushes-Yards (Net)	31-150	29-94
Passing-Yards (Net)	328	257
Passes Att-Comp-Int	37-27-2	26-18-0
Total Offense Plays-Yards	68-478	56-351
Punt Returns-Yards	3-35	0-0
Kickoff Returns-Yards	5-108	5-109
Punts (Number-Avg)	2-30.5	3-54.0
Fumbles-Lost	2-1	0-0
Penalties-Yards	9-75	2-13
Possession Time	33:11	26:49
Sacks by (Number-Yards)	1-3	0-0

Individual Offensive Statistics

Rushing: Cincinnati R. Johnson 24-89; C. Palmer 2-19; K. Watson 2-12; K. Larson 1-11; C. Johnson 1-10; J. Kitna 1-9
New England C. Dillon 22-88; K. Faulk 1-4; T. Brady 5-2; L. Izzo 1-0

Passing: Cincinnati C. Palmer 18-24-2-202; J. Kitna 9-13-1-126
New England T. Brady 18-26-2-260

Receiving: Cincinnati T. Houshmandzadeh 12-145; C. Johnson 5-80; R. Johnson 2-35; K. Washington 2-35; K. Watson 2-15; K. Walter 1-11; R. Kelly 1-5; M. Schobel 1-2; J. Johnson 1-0
New England D. Patten 5-107; D. Branch 3-44; C. Fauria 3-33; T. Brown 2-27; P. Pass 2-22; J. Weaver 2-14; K. Faulk 1-13

Individual Defensive Statistics

Interceptions: Cincinnati none
New England T. Brown 1; A. Samuel 1

Sacks: Cincinnati D. Clemons 1
New England none

Tackles (unassisted-assisted): Cincinnati B. Simmons 6-3; M. Williams 6-1; K. Herring 5-0; D. Clemons 4-1; L. Johnson 4-3; L. Moore 4-0; T. James 3-1; K. Kaesviharn 2-0; C. Miller 2-3; C. Powell 2-0; K. Ratliff 2-1
New England T. Bruschi 12-4; R. Harrison 9-2; R. Gay 5-3; E. Wilson 4-0; W. McGinest 3-3; K. Traylor 3-1; M. Vrabel 3-0; T. Warren 3-0; T. Brown 2-0; L. Izzo 2-0; R. Seymour 2-1

ABOVE: Offensive coordinator Charlie Weis speaks with coaches in the booth. Weis will be leaving the Patriots to be head coach at Notre Dame. *(Matthew West/Boston Herald)*

ABOVE: Patriots Ty Warren (94) and Randall Gay (21) chase down Bengals receiver Chad Johnson in the second quarter after Johnson caught a short pass. *(Matthew West/Boston Herald)*

The offensive star was supposed to be running back Corey Dillon, who was thought to have something to prove against his former team. Instead, the Bengals focused on Dillon and held him to 88 yards on 22 carries.

"It was you guys who hyped it up," said Dillon, who did not conduct interviews last week. "I didn't say a word all week—you know that. And as of today, it's over."

As for the Weis situation, he wasn't made available and the players were forbidden from speaking on the subject by Belichick.

"We can talk about us clinching a playoff berth, though," Fauria said. "That felt good."

But as for the game itself, no one was feeling good.

"We're disappointed in our play," safety Rodney Harrison said. "We just need to play better, that's all. We've got to get better. We will."

Fish Fillet Pats

By Michael Felger, *Boston Herald*

It was a play that was virtually unprecedented in Tom Brady's career. It was a result that no one could have fathomed.

Brady and the Patriots were shocked by the woeful Miami Dolphins on national television, blowing an 11-point lead in the final four minutes and dropping a 29-28 decision at Pro Player Stadium.

The game-winner came with just 1:23 remaining, when Derrius Thompson made a leaping catch over Troy Brown in the end zone on fourth-and-10.

"We blew it," said safety Rodney Harrison, summing up the night.

The loss left the Pats firmly behind the Steelers in the race for the AFC's top seed, but that's not what everyone will be talking about in the next few days. The topic of conversation will be the sequence of events that led to the Pats' losing for only the second time in their last 29 games.

Start with the Brady play. With the Pats leading, 28-23, and facing a third-and-nine deep in their own territory, Brady dropped back in the face of a heavy pass rush. Defensive end

ABOVE: Dolphins wide receiver Derrius Thompson reels in the winning touchdown catch in the fourth quarter, beating Pats defender Troy Brown. *(Matthew West/Boston Herald)*

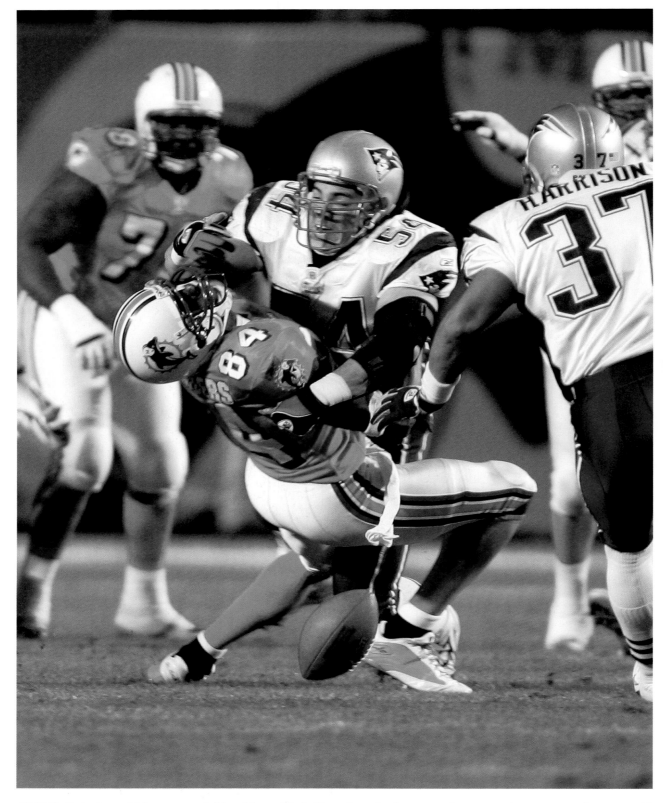

ABOVE: Tedy Bruschi lays a punishing hit on Chris Chambers in the second quarter. *(Matthew West/Boston Herald)*

Jason Taylor got to him and started to drag him down, which is when Brady flipped the ball carelessly down the field. His pass was intercepted by Miami linebacker Brendon Ayanbadejo at the Pats' 21.

Four plays later, the Dolphins had the win.

"I made a terrible decision," Brady said. "You can't expect anything good to happen when you do that. It's a bad play. It's just not a good play. We've got to play better, and it starts with me."

Bill Belichick refused to blame his quarterback.

"We just didn't get it done in any phase. It wasn't any one play," he said. "It was a combination of things."

On the next big play, the Dolphins deserve credit for targeting Brown and going right at him. Lining up the six-foot-two Thompson on the five-foot-ten Brown, quarterback A.J. Feeley never looked anywhere else.

"I feel like I had great position. I didn't finish the play," Brown said. "The guy made a great catch. He was a better player than I was."

Belichick said Brown didn't do much wrong on the play.

"I thought the coverage was good. I thought it was an excellent play," Belichick said. "What am I going to say? The guy made a hell of a catch."

Another big topic in the postgame aftermath was whether the Pats had fallen into a trap considering the Dolphins' woeful 3-11 record and with the Jets next up on the schedule. The Pats said they were prepared for the Dolphins and were ready to play to a high level.

Given the results, that's debatable. The offensive line allowed constant pressure on Brady, who was sacked twice and threw four interceptions. The defense allowed an anemic Dolphins offense to move 68 yards down the field and close the gap on a one-yard Sammy Morris run after Daniel Graham's two-yard touchdown catch had given the Pats a seeming-

	1st	2nd	3rd	4th	Final
New England	7	7	7	7	28
Miami	7	3	7	12	29

Scoring Summary

New England Kevin Faulk 31-yard pass from Tom Brady (Vinatieri kick). Nine plays, 77 yards in 5:01.
Miami Sammy Morris two-yard run (Mare kick). One play, two yards in 0:04.
New England Corey Dillon three-yard run (Vinatieri kick). Twelve plays, 50 yards in 6:48.
Miami Olindo Mare 30-yard field goal. Eleven plays, 58 yards in 5:09.
Miami Travis Minor one-yard run (Mare kick). Ten plays, 43 yards in 4:10.
New England Corey Dillon two-yard pass from Tom Brady (Vinatieri kick). Ten plays, 71 yards in 4:43.
New England Daniel Graham two-yard pass from Tom Brady (Vinatieri kick). Eight plays, 65 yards in 4:57.
Miami Sammy Morris one-yard run (Booker pass from Feeley failed). Seven plays, 68 yards in 1:52.
Miami Derrius Thompson 21-yard pass from A.J. Feeley (Chambers pass from Feeley failed). Four plays, 21 yards in 0:22.

Team Statistics

Category	New England	Miami
First Downs	24	18
Rushes-Yards (Net)	38-166	20-52
Passing-Yards (Net)	156	179
Passes Att-Comp-Int	29-18-4	35-22-0
Total Offense Plays-Yards	69-322	59-231
Punt Returns-Yards	2-17	2-87
Kickoff Returns-Yards	6-111	5-139
Punts (Number-Avg)	4-42.8	6-45.7
Fumbles-Lost	0-0	3-1
Penalties-Yards	4-53	9-67
Possession Time	35:06	24:54
Sacks by (Number-Yards)	4-19	2-15

Individual Offensive Statistics

Rushing: **New England** C. Dillon 26-121; K. Faulk 6-39; P. Pass 4-8; T. Brady 2-minus 2
Miami T. Minor 8-27; S. Morris 9-27; C. Chambers 1-0; A. Feeley 2-minus 2

Passing: **New England** T. Brady 18-29-3-171
Miami A. Feely 22-35-1-198

Receiving: **New England** D. Branch 3-44; D. Patten 4-40; K. Faulk 1-31; D. Graham 3-24; P. Pass 3-17; C. Fauria 1-8; T. Brown 1-6; C. Dillon 2-1
Miami S. Morris 6-46; M. Booker 4-35; D. Thompson 2-31; R. McMichael 4-29; C. Chambers 3-24; B. Gilmore 2-24; D. Lee 1-9

Individual Defensive Statistics

Interceptions: **New England** none
Miami B. Ayanbadejo 1; S. Knight 2; A. Freeman 1

Sacks: **New England** W. McGinest 1; J. Green 1; R. Seymour 1; M. Vrabel .5; R. Phifer .5;
Miami J. Taylor 1; D. Bowens 1

Tackles (unassisted-assisted): **New England** A. Samuel 5-1; W. McGinest 4-2; R. Phifer 4-2; T. Brown 3-2; T. Bruschi 3-1; R. Harrison 3-1; T. Johnson 3-1; D. Davis 2-1; R. Gay 2-0; J. Green 2-0; M. Vrabel 2-1; V. Wilfork 2-1
Miami B. Ayanbadejo 6-5; M. Greenwood 6-5; J. Taylor 6-2; S. Knight 5-4; D. Pope 5-4; A. Freeman 4-0; B. Robinson 2-2; P. Surtain 2-2; J. Zgonina 2-4

ABOVE: Pats coach Bill Belichick reacts with frustration after New England gave up a third-quarter touchdown. Don Davis (51) steals a glance at the scoreboard. *(Matthew West/Boston Herald)*

ly safe 28-17 lead with 3:59 left in the game. The special teams gave up a 71-yard punt return to Wes Welker that gave the Dolphins early life.

But again, the Pats denied the trap scenario.

"I don't think that's what that was about," linebacker Tedy Bruschi said. "Offensively, they made the play. Fourth-and-10."

Said Belichick: "I didn't think it was about intensity. It was about execution."

Overall, the players in the locker room were far from devastated, even though the loss was in many ways devastating.

"The train's moving," tight end Christian Fauria said. "We still have two games left. We can't sit here and feel sorry for ourselves."

ABOVE: Running back Corey Dillon (28) celebrates his second-quarter touchdown with Deion Branch. Dillon scored twice, but it wasn't enough as the Dolphins won, 29-28. *(Matthew West/Boston Herald)*

PATS DOMINATE JETS

By Michael Felger, *Boston Herald*

It was a game that had meaning beyond the AFC seedings, although the Patriots had to be very satisfied where they stood in that regard at the end of the day.

The contest against the Jets was just as much a referendum on the Pats' embattled defense and their suddenly human quarterback. It was just as much a litmus test on where the team was headed with the playoffs looming.

And after three hours of mostly dominant football at Giants Stadium, the Patriots had their answers.

In an overwhelming 23-7 victory, the Pats showed their patchwork secondary still can make the stops and that Tom Brady still can play like a Super Bowl MVP.

Above all, the Pats showed they still are capable of peaking in January, which happens to be the next time they will play a meaningful game. The win assured a No. 2 seed (behind Pittsburgh) and a home playoff game.

Forget for a moment that the Jets stunk in general and quarterback Chad Pennington, in particular, was horrible. As receiver David Givens said, "We needed this."

ABOVE: Tom Brady scrambles on a keeper in the second quarter. *(Matthew West/Boston Herald)*

ABOVE: Mike Vrabel sacks Jets quarterback Chad Pennington. *(Matthew West/Boston Herald)*

To a man, the Pats said they were shocked by last week's last-minute collapse in Miami. That defeat gave them the kick in the pants they needed to play one of their best games this season.

"I thought it was huge. Huge," tight end Christian Fauria said. "After last week, and coming in here, I thought it was one of the biggest games in the regular season we've had in a long, long time."

Added safety Rodney Harrison: "I think all the guys were ticked off, embarrassed, because you just can't blow leads like we did [in Miami] going into the playoffs. You want to have momentum and you want to have some consistency. It was a humbling experience for us, but we came out and we performed like the Patriots should perform."

Start with Brady, who started to hear the catcalls from the fandom for one of the few times in his career. As he so often has done in the past, however, Brady followed up a bad game with a great one, throwing two touchdowns and no interceptions while completing 21-of-32 passes for 264 yards.

"This is why you play the games, to experience the thrill of victory and the agony of defeat," Brady said. "As much as we suffered last week, that's an elated group of guys in that locker room right now."

On the other side, the Jets somehow were unable to take advantage of the Pats' banged-up secondary, which still was without Ty Law and featured way too much of Earthwind Moreland and Troy Brown. The Pats loaded on Curtis Martin, and it turned out to be no privilege watching Pennington try to pick up the slack. The Jets didn't start picking on Moreland until it was too late, and all they managed was a meaningless Santana Moss touchdown catch.

While Brady and Corey Dillon were being smart and productive on offense and Tedy Bruschi and Eugene Wilson (both had intercep-

	1st	2nd	3rd	4th	Final
New England	0	13	3	7	23
New York	0	0	0	7	7

Scoring Summary
New England Adam Vinatieri 28-yard field goal. Fifteen plays, 59 yards in 7:18.
New England Daniel Graham 16-yard pass from Tom Brady (Vinatieri kick). Eight plays, 86 yards in 4:12.
New England Adam Vinatieri 29-yard field goal. Seven plays, 32 yards in 1:06.
New England Adam Vinatieri 26-yard field goal. Thirteen plays, 79 yards in 7:21.
New England Deion Branch six-yard pass from Tom Brady (Vinatieri kick). Four plays, 15 yards in 2:13.
New York Santana Moss 15-yard pass from Chad Pennington (Brien kick). Nine plays, 67 yards in 3:04.

Team Statistics
Category	New England	New York
First Downs	21	17
Rushes-Yards (Net)	38-114	18-46
Passing-Yards (Net)	258	233
Passes Att-Comp-Int	32-21-0	36-22-2
Total Offense Plays-Yards	71-372	57-279
Punt Returns-Yards	3-23	3-18
Kickoff Returns-Yards	2-38	5-97
Punts (Number-Avg)	4-36.8	5-31.4
Fumbles-Lost	2-0	2-1
Penalties-Yards	3-25	4-20
Possession Time	35:48	24:12
Sacks by (Number-Yards)	3-19	1-6

Individual Offensive Statistics
Rushing: **New England** C. Dillon 29-89; P. Pass 4-17; R. Abdullah 1-5; T. Brady 4-3
New York C. Martin 13-33; C. Pennington 3-7; L. Jordan 2-6

Passing: **New England** T. Brady 21-32-2-264
New York C. Pennington 22-36-1-252

Receiving: **New England** D. Branch 7-82; D. Givens 2-64; C. Fauria 3-44; P. Pass 5-32; D. Graham 2-30; C. Dillon 2-12
New York J. McCareins 5-76; W. Chrebet 4-51; C. Martin 5-44; S. Moss 2-32; J. Cotchery 1-18; L. Jordan 3-16; J. Sowell 2-15

Individual Defensive Statistics
Interceptions: **New England** T. Bruschi 1; E. Wilson 1
New York none

Sacks: **New England** M. Vrabel 1; R. Colvin 1; J. Green 1
New York J. Vilma 1

Tackles (unassisted-assisted): **New England** T. Bruschi 6-2; T. Johnson 6-0; D. Davis 4-1; A. Samuel 4-1; M. Vrabel 4-1; R. Harrison 3-2; W. McGinest 3-0; T. Banta-Cain 2-1; T. Brown 2-0; E. Moreland 2-1; C. Morton 2-0; T. Warren 2-1; V. Wilfork 2-2
New York E. Coleman 9-1; R. Tongue 7-1; J. Vilma 7-4; D. Barrett 5-0; E. Barton 5-1; B. Thomas 4-3; J. Ferguson 3-1; T. Johnson 3-1; D. Abraham 2-1; J. Cotchery 2-0; V. Hobson 2-1; D. McClover 2-0; J. McGraw 2-1

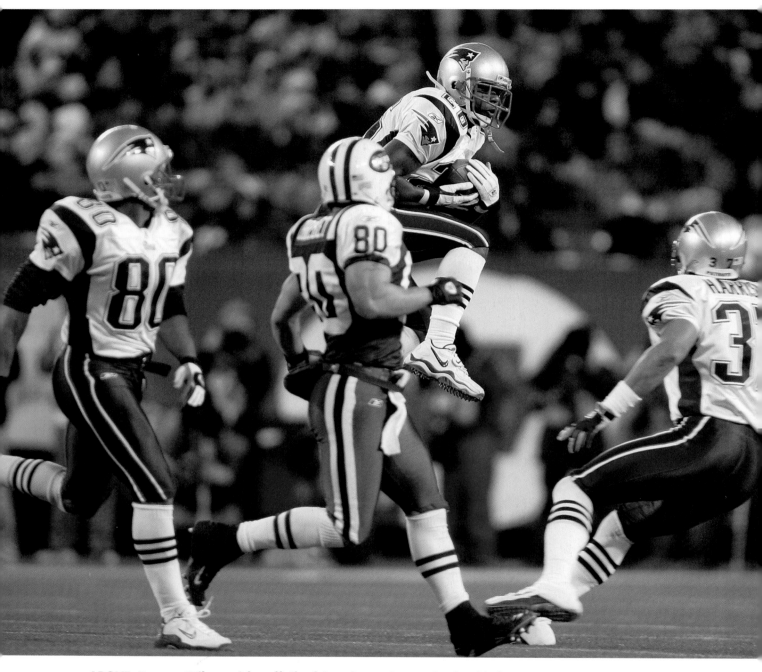

ABOVE: Eugene Wilson picks off Chad Pennington's pass in the third quarter, which led to Deion Branch's touchdown. *(Matthew West/Boston Herald)*

tions) were doing the job on defense, the special teams closed the gates on kick coverage. In other words, the Pats were most of the things they haven't been this month.

"A lot of guys stepped up and showed a lot of toughness," coach Bill Belichick said. "This was the kind of game we needed—in all three phases."

ABOVE: Corey Dillon breaks a tackle by Jets Eric Barton en route to a big gain on a short pass in the second quarter. Dillon contributed 89 rushing yards to the Patriots' win. *(Matthew West/Boston Herald)*

STAYING SHARP

By Rich Thompson, *Boston Herald*

Patriots inside linebacker Tedy Bruschi didn't let the significance of the 21-7 victory over the San Francisco 49ers alter his frantic style. Even though the Patriots had already locked up the second seed in the AFC playoffs and a guaranteed first-round bye, Bruschi attacked the 49ers as if the Patriots were fighting for the final wild card spot.

Bruschi led the Patriots with 15 tackles to improve his season total to 129. He came up one short of the season-high 16 tackles he logged in the Patriots' loss at Pittsburgh on Halloween. Bruschi's mantra is full-tilt, full-time, and it didn't matter that the 49ers were an aimless, mismanaged club with a 2-13 record.

"This game here, we played the whole game because that's just the way we are around here," said Bruschi. "There is something about rest, but we were in a tight game and we just want to win football games. That's the bottom line and that's the situation we were in. This was a game a lot of people didn't look at as important, but in this locker room we wanted to win the game."

ABOVE: Rodney Harrison (37) and Don Davis level San Francisco's Curtis Conway (89) during third-quarter action. *(Stuart Cahill/Boston Herald)*

ABOVE: Deion Branch just manages to keep it in the end zone for an eight-yard touchdown in the third quarter. (Nancy Lane/Boston Herald)

Bruschi had to perform at his optimum level because 49ers tailback Kevan Barlow refused to roll over, despite the circumstances. The six-foot-one, 238-pound Barlow exhibits a running style similar to Pittsburgh's Jerome Bettis, and he isn't shy about making middle linebackers earn their money.

Barlow continued to run hard even when it was obvious the 49ers were on their way to their 14th lost cause. Barlow finished the game with 103 yards on 25 carries and he earned Bruschi's respect with that effort.

"I've watched him, I've followed him and he's always a guy that runs hard," Bruschi said. "He was running hard, and I think our guys were looking forward to the chance to put some licks on him.

"He's a big, physical runner and he gets up and lets you know that he's physical. He'll say a couple of things, but hey, we're physical too, and we kept hitting him."

Patriots strong safety Rodney Harrison is a defensive back with a linebacker's mentality and the numbers to substantiate that approach. Harrison finished second to Bruschi with nine tackles and improved his team lead to a career-high 139.

"That [49ers record] never entered into it," Harrison said. "The fact is we were on all cylinders, communicating and not missing tackles.

"From a mental standpoint, we made all the adjustments. From a defensive standpoint, we had guys out there flying around, knocking balls down and making tackles. We made sure we played hard."

	1st	2nd	3rd	4th	Final
San Francisco	7	0	0	0	7
New England	0	7	7	7	21

Scoring Summary
San Francisco Steve Bush four-yard pass from Ken Dorsey (Peterson kick). Five plays, 22 yards in 2:21.
New England Mike Vrabel one-yard pass from Tom Brady (Vinatieri kick). Eight plays, 71 yards in 4:20.
New England Deion Branch eight-yard pass from Tom Brady (Vinatieri kick). Four plays, 51 yards in 1:51.
New England Corey Dillon six-yard run (Vinatieri kick). Nine plays, 66 yards in 4:36.

Team Statistics

Category	San Francisco	New England
First Downs	15	23
Rushes-Yards (Net)	35-135	28-174
Passing-Yards (Net)	183	231
Passes Att-Comp-Int	29-18-0	34-23-1
Total Offense Plays-Yards	65-318	63-405
Punt Returns-Yards	1-10	4-8
Kickoff Returns-Yards	4-97	2-50
Punts (Number-Avg)	5-42.8	4-38.2
Fumbles-Lost	2-2	3-2
Penalties-Yards	7-64	4-37
Possession Time	30:48	29:12
Sacks by (Number-Yards)	1-5	1-6

Individual Offensive Statistics
Rushing: **San Francisco** K. Barlow 25-103; M. Hicks 10-32.
New England C. Dillon 14-116; C. Cobbs 5-20; P. Pass 4-16; B. Johnson 1-11; R. Abdullah 2-5; T. Brady 1-3; R. Davey 1-3.

Passing: **San Francisco** K. Dorsey 18-29-1-189.
New England T. Brady 22-30-2-226; R. Davey 1-4-0-10.

Receiving: **San Francisco** R. Woods 3-76; C. Conway 4-44; E. Johnson 3-28; K. Barlow 2-11; S. Bush 2-10; M. Hicks 2-10; C. Wilson 1-7; A. Walker 1-3.
New England J. Weaver 4-62; C. Fauria 3-37; D. Givens 2-30; D. Patten 1-23; D. Branch 3-22; P. Pass 5-22; C. Dillon 1-18; B. Johnson 2-15; T. Brown 1-6; M. Vrabel 1-1.

Individual Defensive Statistics
Interceptions: **San Francisco** D. Carpenter 1.
New England none

Sacks: **San Francisco** J. Engelberger 1.
New England W. McGinest 1

Tackles (unassisted-assisted): **San Francisco** J. Ulbrich 9-3; T. Parrish 6-1; D. Smith 6-3; S. Rasheed 5-2; T. Brown 3-0; D. Carpenter 3-2; M. Hicks 3-0; S. Spencer 3-0; A. Williams 3-0; J. Hanson 2-0; J. Williams 2-1; B. Young 2-0.
New England T. Bruschi 9-6; R. Gay 4-0; J. Green 4-3; R. Harrison 4-5; T. Johnson 4-4; T. Banta-Cain 3-3; D. Davis 3-1; W. McGinest 3-1; R. Phifer 3-1; K. Traylor 3-0; T. Warren 3-1; E. Alexander 2-0; E. Moreland 2-0; A. Samuel 2-0; V. Wilfork 2-3.

SMASHMOUTH PATS

By Michael Felger, *Boston Herald*

How many times do people have to see it before they believe it?

Physical football wins in the postseason. Finesse doesn't.

When will they finally learn?

Offense wins games. Defense wins championships.

The Patriots drove home those facts in overwhelming fashion, smothering record-setting quarterback Peyton Manning and the Colts, 20-3, at Gillette Stadium to advance to the AFC Championship Game in Pittsburgh.

"What this [win] says is that the experts are wrong," defensive end Jarvis Green said. "That's what it says."

Indeed, it seemed the entire NFL community had once again fallen in love with Manning and the high-flying Colts, forgetting that dome teams built on speed rarely go into the elements against teams built on power and come out victorious. The Pats are bigger, stronger and tougher than the Colts. Why did people forget that?

"The [Colts] don't seem to like it too much when teams get physical with them," safety

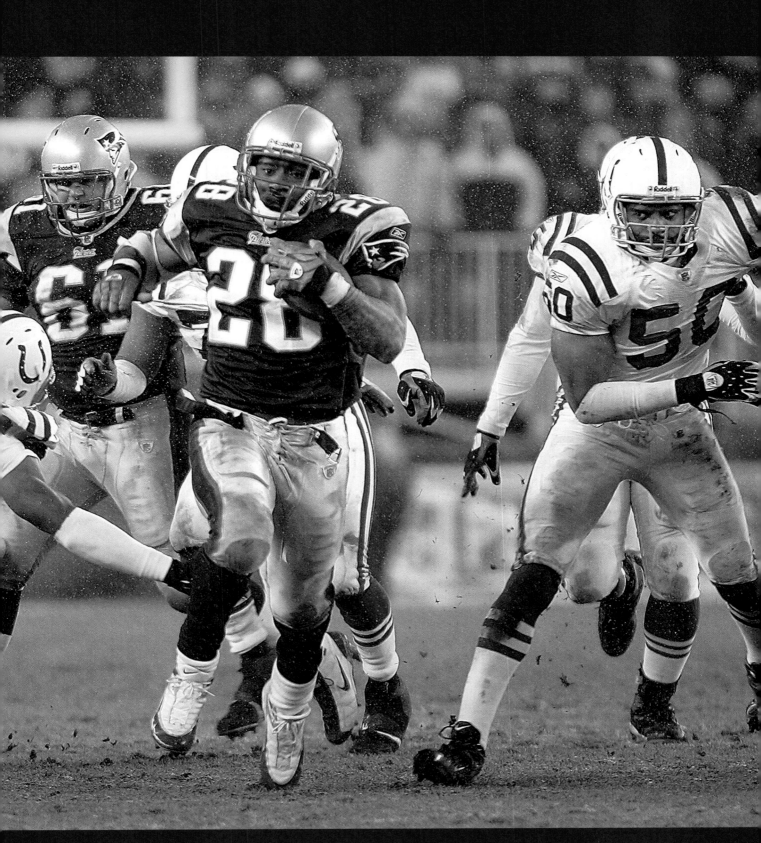

ABOVE: Running back Corey Dillon breaks into the open for a huge gain in the second quarter. Dillon rushed for 144 yards against the Colts. *(Matthew West/Boston Herald)*

ABOVE: Eugene Wilson breaks up the pass to Brandon Stokley in second-quarter action.
(Stuart Cahill/Boston Herald)

Eugene Wilson said. "A lot of people doubted us, but we didn't doubt ourselves. We knew we'd win the game."

The outcome was yet another remarkable feat in the tenure of coach Bill Belichick. Playing without his two starting cornerbacks (Ty Law and Tyrone Poole) and his best defensive player (Richard Seymour), the Pats played hands-on football in the secondary, disrupting the timing of the Colts receivers while forcing Manning into a bevy of short, possession throws. The Colts rarely threatened, crossing the 50-yard line just four times. Meanwhile, the Pats tackled like maniacs, forcing three turnovers.

But the Pats didn't save the smashmouth approach just for the defense. On offense, the Pats ran the ball down the Colts' throats, with Corey Dillon churning for 144 yards and Kevin Faulk gashing the middle for 56. The more plays Dillon and Faulk made, the more offensive coordinator Charlie Weis went to the run. And the result was three remarkable, clock-eating drives that decided the game.

The first lasted 16 plays, consumed 9:07 and resulted in an Adam Vinatieri field goal that gave the Pats a 3-0 lead. The second lasted 13 plays, consumed 8:16 and ended in a Tom Brady five-yard touchdown pass to David Givens. The final march lasted 14 plays, took up 7:24 and resulted in a Brady sneak.

Sitting in the locker room with a 6-3 lead at the half, Belichick challenged his players to dig deep, and that's what they did. They finished the game without a turnover and a whopping lead in time of possession (37:43 to 22:17).

"It was a tremendous effort," Belichick said. "We came into the locker room [at halftime] knowing we'd need to have our best 30 minutes of football, and I really think we got it. ... It was an awesome performance."

Dillon was the star of the game, and thanks to him the Pats were able to take some pressure off their offensive line, which had trouble pro-

	1st	2nd	3rd	4th	Final
Indianapolis	0	3	0	0	3
New England	0	6	7	7	20

Scoring Summary
New England Adam Vinatieri 24-yard field goal. Sixteen plays, 78 yards in 9:07.
New England Adam Vinatieri 31-yard field goal. Six plays, 48 yards in 1:26.
Indianapolis Mike Vanderjagt 23-yard field goal. Eleven plays, 67 yards in 1:52.
New England David Givens five-yard pass from Tom Brady (Vinatieri kick). Fifteen plays, 87 yards in 8:16.
New England Tom Brady one-yard run (Vinatieri kick). Fourteen plays, 94 yards in 7:24.

Team Statistics
Category	Indianapolis	New England
First Downs	18	21
Rushes-Yards (Net)	15-46	39-210
Passing-Yards (Net)	230	115
Passes Att-Comp-Int	42-27-1	27-18-0
Total Offense Plays-Yards	58-276	69-325
Punt Returns-Yards	0-0	2-28
Kickoff Returns-Yards	4-58	1-15
Punts (Number-Avg)	6-40.7	5-39.0
Fumbles-Lost	3-2	0-0
Penalties-Yards	4-44	5-35
Possession Time	22:17	37:43
Sacks by (Number-Yards)	3-29	1-8

Individual Offensive Statistics
Rushing: **Indianapolis** E. James 14-39; P. Manning 1-7
New England C. Dillon 23-144; K. Faulk 11-56; T. Brady 4-6; D. Branch 1-4

Passing: **Indianapolis** P. Manning 27-42-0-238
New England T. Brady 18-27-1-144

Receiving: **Indianapolis** E. James 7-69; B. Stokley 8-64; M. Harrison 5-44; R. Wayne 3-35; D. Clark 2-26; M. Pollard 1-2; D. Rhodes 1-minus 2
New England D. Givens 4-26; C. Dillon 5-17; C. Fauria 1-17; D. Branch 1-15; P. Pass 1-14; T. Brown 2-13; D. Patten 1-12; K. Faulk 1-11; D. Graham 1-10; B. Johnson 1-9

Individual Defensive Statistics
Interceptions: **Indianapolis** none
New England R. Harrison 1

Sacks: **Indianapolis** M. Reagor 1; L. Tripplett 1; D. Freeney 1
New England M. Vrabel 1

Tackles (unassisted-assisted): **Indianapolis** I. Bashir 6-3; M. Reagor 6-1; D. Thornton 6-1; L. Tripplett 6-0; J. Jefferson 5-0; J. Williams 5-1; G. Brackett 4-0; C. June 4-9; J. David 3-0; V. Hutchins 3-3; B. Sanders 3-4; M. Doss 2-1; N. Harper 2-1
New England R. Harrison 8-2; M. Vrabel 6-2; R. Gay 5-0; T. Bruschi 4-3; R. Phifer 3-0; A. Samuel 3-0; T. Brown 2-1; J. Cherry 2-0; W. McGinest 2-0; D. Reid 2-1; V. Wilfork 2-0

ABOVE: Kevin Faulk cuts upfield against Indy cornerback Nicholas Harper (25). *(Nancy Lane/Boston Herald)*

tecting Brady in front of defensive end Dwight Freeney and the Colts' hard-charging line.

"What really did it for us is we opened up that running game and got Corey going," tackle Matt Light said. "A lot of good things happen when he's having a good game. That's just a great win for us. We're feeling pretty high right now."

The Pats played the lack-of-respect card to the hilt last week, with Rodney Harrison going so far as to say he lost sleep because of it. The week began with Colts kicker Mike Vanderjagt

nearly guaranteeing victory. It ended with Vanderjagt providing the only points the Colts would have.

"The best thing that happened was that Vanderjagt scored three points," Green said. "He'll have to go back and work on that."

That was the extent of the postgame trash talk for the Pats. For them, the focus immediately turned to avenging their October loss at the Steelers.

Said Brady: "We need to get our lunch pails and go right back to work."

ABOVE: Tedy Bruschi celebrates his fumble recovery in the second quarter. *(Matthew West/Boston Herald)*

#28 COREY DILLON

With 10 minutes left in the game, the frozen yet appreciative Foxboro faithful took up the chant. Tens of thousands of them shouted—"Corey! Corey!"—as he trotted off the field after hauling in a Tom Brady pass for a first down.

"Whenever the crowd is into the game like that, it's special," said Dillon. "I think the whole team was pretty pumped up about it. It means you're out there doing something good. I heard it, I appreciate it. Thank you much."

And 10 minutes after the game his jubilant teammates had adopted yet another mantra. By the time Dillon emerged from the shower he had a new moniker: "Clock-Killin' Dillon!" they kept shouting. "Clock-Killin' Dillon."

If you were looking for an explanation for the Patriots' nearly 2-1 time of possession edge over Indy in the playoff win, Exhibit A was wearing No. 28.

Dillon ran the ball 23 times for 144 yards, the second-highest total in Patriots postseason history. He caught five passes for another 17 yards, and when he wasn't running or catching, protected Tom Brady by picking up blitzers.

And he chewed up minutes even more effectively than he did yards.

He did everything, in short, except score a touchdown, and in fact he did that, too. When the Patriots gambled and went for it early in the second quarter, Dillon scored on fourth-and-goal from the one, only to have the TD wiped out when Matt Light was flagged for a false start. The Pats had to settle for a field goal.

"It just came off the board," shrugged Dillon. "What am I supposed to do about it? At least we got three out of it."

At 30 years of age he was playing in his first-ever postseason game. Time and again he would seemingly be hemmed in by the Colts' defenders, only to bounce out of the pile and take off in a new direction with white jerseys in hot pursuit.

"There was a couple of opportunities when I backed into a couple of players, came out of it, and made a cut and got some yards. It's just a matter of seeing the field, keeping my head on a swivel, keeping my legs moving and getting upfield with the ball," Dillon recalled.

"We wanted to control the clock a little bit. We didn't want to put the ball in their hands too many times. That's a hot offense and they can put up points in a second if you give them the ball."

Shortly after the crowd erupted in the "Corey! Corey!" chant, Dillon trotted back out onto the field. He got the call on third-and-eight at the 28-yard line, plowed into the middle, and did what he'd been doing all night. Colts defenders swarmed on him from every direction, and the next thing anybody saw was Dillon squirming out of the pile and lighting out for the left sideline.

By the time Indianapolis safety Idrees Bashir knocked him out of bounds he'd gotten to the one. Brady scored on a quarterback sneak on the next play to make it 20-3, and it was time to stick a fork in the Colts.

"That," Brady said, "was a huge run."

"Corey set the tone—as he has all year," said Brady, who described Dillon as "the best running back in the league."

"He plays with so much heart and effort, it's just contagious," said Pats tight end Christian Fauria. "Even when we miss blocks, he's making tacklers miss and stiff-arming guys. He's just the heart of the offense."

For seven long seasons he had labored in Cincinnati, meaning that mid-January football was a new experience to him.

"To actually be in the playoffs and playing for something that means something, I'm going to cherish it," Dillon said.

—By George Kimball, *Boston Herald*

Position: *Running Back*
Height: *6'1"*
Weight: *225*
Born: *10/24/74*
College: *Washington*
NFL Experience: *8 years*

Stuart Cahill/Boston Herald

FLORIDA-BOUND!

By Michael Felger, *Boston Herald*

Last week, the Patriots smothered the most prolific, high-flying offense in football. The next week, they traveled to the other end of the spectrum and dissected one of the NFL's most physical, defensive-minded teams.

What's left?

History.

For the third time in four years, the Patriots punched their ticket to the Super Bowl, beating the Pittsburgh Steelers, 41-27, at frigid Heinz Field in the AFC Championship Game. Awaiting them in Jacksonville, Fla., will be the Philadelphia Eagles, who will be going for their first-ever Super Bowl championship.

The Pats already own two of those, and a win over the Eagles would give them their third since the 2001 season. It would be a run of excellence equaled only by the 1991-94 Cowboys, who won three Super Bowls in a four-year span.

"To see the job the players and the coaches did the last two weeks is just unbelievable," said owner Robert Kraft, who watched his team post a 20-3 win over Indianapolis in the divisional round. "These two efforts together, with all the things we've had going against us—this

ABOVE: David Givens hoists Deion Branch into the air after Branch's 60-yard touchdown catch. Branch scored a running touchdown against the Steelers later in the game. *(Michael Seamans/Boston Herald)*

ABOVE: Jarvis Green takes down Steelers quarterback Ben Roethlisberger in the first quarter. Roethlisberger was sacked once and threw three interceptions. *(Michael Seamans/Boston Herald)*

is one of the finest coaching, and player, executions I've [seen]. It's been pretty special."

Added Corey Dillon: "We made it. It's a beautiful feeling."

Dillon figured to be a central figure in the game, but the Steelers' front seven gave the Pats only marginal running room all night. That left it up to Tom Brady to go up top, and he delivered with a stellar 207-yard, two-touchdown, no interception evening. He's now 8-0 career in the postseason.

"There are a bunch of guys who are 8-0 in this locker room," said Brady. "I'm just included."

Brady was being modest, as usual. Just like his coach.

"We got a few breaks along the way," said Bill Belichick, who raised his playoff record to 9-1, tied with Vince Lombardi for the best postseason winning percentage in NFL history. "The credit goes to the players."

This was a game of big plays for the Pats, including a 60-yard touchdown catch by Deion Branch, an 87-yard interception return for a touchdown by Rodney Harrison, a 25-yard scoring run by Dillon and a 23-yard scoring reverse by Branch to salt the game away late in the fourth quarter.

The result gave the Steelers their fourth home loss in the AFC title game in five tries under Bill Cowher, and after the Pats stormed out to leads of 10-0 and 24-3 in the first half, the frenzied, sellout crowd knew another disappointment was at hand. Ballyhooed rookie quarterback Ben Roethlisberger played like one, throwing three interceptions (two to Eugene Wilson).

"Did we shut them up? What do you think?" asked incredulous cornerback Asante Samuel. "They tried to get talking a little bit, but they couldn't."

The Pats clearly had revenge on their minds following their 34-20 loss in Pittsburgh on October 31.

	1st	2nd	3rd	4th	Final
New England	10	14	7	10	41
Pittsburgh	3	0	14	10	27

Scoring Summary

New England Adam Vinatieri 48-yard field goal. Five plays, 18 yards in 2:13.
New England Deion Branch 60-yard pass from Tom Brady (Vinatieri kick). One play, 60 yards in 0:09.
Pittsburgh Jeff Reed 43-yard field goal. Five plays, 23 yards in 2:10.
New England David Givens 9-yard pass from Tom Brady (Vinatieri kick). Five plays, 70 yards in 2:52.
New England Rodney Harrison 87-yard interception return (Vinatieri kick).
Pittsburgh Jerome Bettis five-yard run (Reed kick). Five plays, 56 yards in 2:39.
New England Corey Dillon 25-yard run (Vinatieri kick). Seven plays, 69 yards in 3:27.
Pittsburgh Hines Ward 30-yard pass from Ben Roethlisberger (Reed kick). Ten plays, 60 yards in 4:52.
Pittsburgh Jeff Reed 20-yard field goal 13:29. Six plays, 53 yards in 2:14.
New England Adam Vinatieri 31-yard field goal. Ten plays, 49 yards in 5:26.
New England Deion Branch 23-yard run (Vinatieri kick). Ten plays, 55 yards in 5:06.
Pittsburgh Plaxico Burress seven-yard pass from Ben Roethlisberger (Reed kick). Six plays, 61 yards in 1:31.

Team Statistics

Category	New England	Pittsburgh
First Downs	18	19
Rushes-Yards (Net)	32-126	37-163
Passing-Yards (Net)	196	225
Passes Att-Comp-Int	21-14-0	24-14-3
Total Offense Plays-Yards	55-322	62-388
Punt Returns-Yards	2-6	3-40
Kickoff Returns-Yards	5-107	8-115
Punts (Number-Avg)	4-40.2	3-43.0
Fumbles-Lost	1-0	2-1
Penalties-Yards	1-5	2-20
Possession Time	28:29	31:31
Sacks by (Number-Yards)	1-1	2-11

Individual Offensive Statistics

Rushing: New England C. Dillon 24-73; D. Branch 2-37; K. Faulk 3-20; T. Brady 2-minus 2; D. Givens 1-minus 2
Pittsburgh J. Bettis 17-64; B. Roethlisberger 5-45; V. Haynes 5-28; D. Staley 10-26

Passing: New England T. Brady 14-21-2-207
Pittsburgh B. Roethlisberger 14-24-2-226

Receiving: New England D. Branch 4-116; D. Givens 5-59; T. Brown 1-11; C. Fauria 1-9; D. Patten 1-8; C. Dillon 1-5; D. Graham 1-minus 1
Pittsburgh H. Ward 5-109; A. Randle El 3-52; P. Burress 3-37; V. Haynes 1-14; J. Tuman 1-8; W. Rasby 1-6

Individual Defensive Statistics

Interceptions: New England E. Wilson 2; R. Harrison 1
Pittsburgh none

Sacks: New England J. Green 1
Pittsburgh J. Porter 1; C. Haggans 1

Tackles (unassisted-assisted): New England R. Harrison 10-2; T. Bruschi 8-1; T. Warren 6-2; M. Vrabel 5-1; T. Johnson 4-4; J. Green 3-2; A. Samuel 3-1; R. Abdullah 2-0; T. Brown 2-1; J. Cherry 2-1; H. Poteat 2-0; E. Wilson 2-2
Pittsburgh T. Polamalu 6-1; J. Farrior 5-5; L. Foote 4-1; J. Porter 4-2; W. Williams 4-3; C. Hope 3-2; A. Smith 3-2; R. Colclough 2-0; C. Haggans 2-4; C. Kriewaldt 2-3

ABOVE: Rodney Harrison is off to the races on this second-quarter, 87-yard interception return for a touch-down. *(Matthew West/Boston Herald)*

"What happened the first game, that wasn't us," said defensive end Jarvis Green, who had another solid game filling in for injured defensive end Richard Seymour. "Today we played together and made the fewest mistakes. We all communicated and it showed."

As for matching up with the hard-hitting Steelers, the Pats more than held their own.

"Everyone said they were the most physical team, but that's our MO: to be physical, play smart football and make plays when we have to," Harrison said. "And that's what we did."

So the Pats are once again headed to the NFL's promised land. If they haven't already recorded their place in NFL history, then a win over the Eagles will cement it.

The players, however, had more immediate concerns on their minds.

"I need to see some sun!" said tight end Christian Fauria. "I'm sick of this cold and snow. I want to wear some shorts. Let's go!"

ABOVE: Tedy Bruschi hoists the AFC Championship trophy after the Pats defeated the Steelers, 41-27.
(Matthew West/Boston Herald)

DYNASTY!

By Michael Felger, *Boston Herald*

Some may want to debate it and some may feel the need to qualify it, but no matter how you get there, the truth is now self-evident.

The Patriots are the NFL's newest dynasty.

Not that the Pats would even utter that word following their 24-21 victory over the Philadelphia Eagles in Super Bowl XXXIX at Alltel Stadium. Even after the fact, the Pats remained true to themselves.

"We've never used that word," said departing offensive coordinator Charlie Weis. "But three out of four ain't bad."

Certainly not. The victory allowed the Pats to join the 1992-95 Dallas Cowboys as only the second team in NFL history to win three Super Bowls in a four-year span. And Bill Belichick supplanted Vince Lombardi with the best post-season winning percentage in league history, a feat that was celebrated by a ceremonial ice water shower that doused both Belichick and his father, Steve.

"That was just something we hadn't been able to do," said linebacker Tedy Bruschi. "The last two [Super Bowls] came down to last-second field goals."

ABOVE: Head coach Bill Belichick celebrates with the Patriots after Rodney Harrison's interception in the final seconds sealed the game. *(David Goldman/Boston Herald)*

BELOW: Asante Samuel holds Terrell Owens to a short gain on this third-quarter reception. The Pats' defense shut Owens down and did not allow him to score. *(Matthew West/Boston Herald)*

The unquestioned pregame star of the week was the Eagles' Terrell Owens, and he proved to be a big factor (nine catches, 122 yards). But he wasn't even the best wide receiver on the field last night. That distinction went to the Pats' Deion Branch, who tied a Super Bowl record with 11 receptions (for 133 yards) and was named the game's MVP.

Putting aside some personal worries, Tom Brady was shaky early but solid later, finishing with two touchdowns and a 110.2 quarterback rating. Donovan McNabb had huge numbers (357 yards, three touchdowns) but he threw some balls that were so bad they were hard to fathom. He threw three interceptions and was sacked four times.

Part of that performance was the result of a trademark defensive wrinkle from the Pats. Playing with only two down-linemen and five linebackers for much of the night, McNabb never knew where the rush was coming from and was mostly contained within the pocket.

"The key was confusing him," said linebacker Willie McGinest. "Anytime you let a guy sit back there and throw passes, he'll pick you apart."

That left the Pats susceptible to the run—but they didn't care. As one veteran said: "We knew they couldn't run on us, no matter how we lined up. They just couldn't."

The Pats also played the game with their customary edge, mocking Owens' touchdown dance after David Givens' four-yard touchdown catch tied the score at 7-7 in the second quarter and after Mike Vrabel's spectacular, juggling touchdown grab gave the Pats a 14-7 lead early in the third quarter.

"We heard a lot of stuff from there. We just had to rub it in their face," said Givens. "When people talk that much, that's what you have to do."

	1st	2nd	3rd	4th	Final
New England	0	7	7	10	24
Philadelphia	0	7	7	7	21

Scoring Summary

Philadelphia L.J. Smith six-yard pass from Donovan McNabb (Akers kick). Nine plays, 81 yards in 4:36.
New England David Givens four-yard pass from Tom Brady (Vinatieri kick). Seven plays, 37 yards in 3:15.
New England Mike Vrabel two-yard pass from Tom Brady (Vinatieri kick). Nine plays, 69 yards in 3:56.
Philadelphia Brian Westbrook 10-yard pass from Donovan McNabb (Akers kick). Ten plays, 74 yards in 4:17.
New England Corey Dillon two-yard run (Vinatieri kick). Nine plays, 66 yards in 4:51.
New England Adam Vinatieri 22-yard field goal. Eight plays, 43 yards in 3:49.
Philadelphia Greg Lewis 30-yard pass from Donovan McNabb (Akers kick). Thirteen plays, 79 yards in 3:52.

Team Statistics

Category	New England	Philadelphia
First Downs	21	24
Rushes-Yards (Net)	28-112	17-45
Passing Yards (Net)	219	324
Passes Att-Comp-Int	33-23-0	51-30-3
Total Offense Plays-Yards	63-331	72-369
Punt Returns-Yards	4-26	3-19
Kickoff Returns-Yards	3-61	5-114
Punts (Number-Avg)	7-45.1	5-42.8
Fumbles-Lost	1-1	2-1
Penalties-Yards	7-47	3-35
Possession Time	31:37	28:33
Sacks by (Number-Yards)	4-33	2-17

Individual Offensive Statistics

Rushing **New England** C. Dillon 18-75; K. Faulk 8-38; P. Pass 1-0; T. Brady 1-minus 1
Philadelphia B. Westbrook 15-44; D. Levens 1-1; D. McNabb 1-0

Passing: **New England** T. Brady 23-33-2-236
Philadelphia D. McNabb 30-51-3-357

Receiving: **New England** D. Branch 11-133; C. Dillon 3-31; K. Faulk 2-27; D. Givens 3-19; T. Brown 2-17; D. Graham 1-7; M. Vrabel 1-2
Philadelphia T. Owens 9-122; T. Pinkston 4-82; B. Westbrook 7-60; G. Lewis 4-53; L. Smith 4-27; F. Mitchell 1-11; J. Parry 1-2

Individual Defensive Statistics

Interceptions: **New England** Harrison 2, Bruschi
Philadelphia none

Sacks: **New England** Harrison 1; Bruschi 1; Vrabel 1; Seymour 1
Philadelphia Burgess 1; TEAM 1

Tackles (unassisted-assisted): **New England** R. Gay 10-0; R. Harrison 7-0; T. Bruschi 6-1; A. Samuel 4-0; R. Phifer 3-0; D. Reid 3-0; E. Wilson 3-0; M. Chatham 2-0; T. Johnson 2-1; W. McGinest 2-0; R. Seymour 2-0; M. Vrabel 2-2
Philadelphia M. Lewis 5-1; K. Adams 4-1; B. Dawkins 4-1; J. Trotter 4-0; M. Ware 4-0; S. Brown 3-1; D. Burgess 3-1; R. Hood 3-0; D. Jones 2-0; M. Labinjo 2-0; G. Lewis 2-0; S. Rayburn 2-0; I. Reese 2-0; L. Sheppard 2-1; M. Simoneau 2-0; D. Walker 2-1

ABOVE: Deion Branch makes a miraculous catch from behind Sheldon Brown. Branch tied the Super Bowl record with 11 receptions and was named MVP. (Stuart Cahill/Boston Herald)

ABOVE: Tom Brady makes a pass in the third quarter. Brady completed 23 passes for 236 yards and two touchdowns. *(Matthew West/Boston Herald)*

The Pats were clearly agitated by the Eagles' talkative style, which safety Rodney Harrison repeatedly referred to as "side shows and antics." Belichick also left his players with a

parting shot at the end of their pregame meeting at the team hotel.

"He just said, 'Go out and make history,'" said one player. "Then at the end he was like, 'Oh yeah. I've heard they've already planned

ABOVE: After stopping Donovan McNabb for a loss in the third quarter, Richard Seymour does the chicken dance, much to the chagrin of the Eagles. *(Matthew West/Boston Herald)*

their parade. The route and everything. I just thought you should know.'"

Even the Pats ownership got in the act, recalling the trash talk from Eagles receiver Freddie Mitchell a week earlier.

"How many catches did Freddie Mitchell have?" asked vice chairman Jonathan Kraft.

The number was one.

The number for the Pats is now three—and counting.

BELOW: Tedy Bruschi sacks Donovan McNabb. McNabb was sacked four times and threw three interceptions. *(Nancy Lane/Boston Herald)*

BELOW: Corey Dillon eludes Eagles tackle Hollis Thomas. Dillon rushed for 75 yards and scored on a short run in the fourth quarter. *(Matthew West/Boston Herald)*

ABOVE: Coach Bill Belichick holds the Lombardi trophy after his Patriots defended their title against the Philadelphia Eagles. *(Nancy Lane/Boston Herald)*

#83 DEION BRANCH

Deion Branch began his Super Bowl with a pregame routine he established long ago and another man's premonition.

"The day before a game I call all my coaches from college and high school, little league," Branch said. "I still owe thanks to the people who helped me reach that level. Scott Pioli saw me this morning and told me he'd had a dream I'd have a big game."

Good grief. Patriots management knows all even when unconscious. Branch ended Super Bowl XXXIX window-shopping for Cadillacs. He was named MVP after the Pats' 24-21 win over the Philadelphia Eagles. The wideout tied a Super Bowl record by making 11 receptions for 133 yards. This means former coach Coleman Kemp will get a follow-up call from Branch sometime today.

"He was my offensive coordinator in high school [in Albany, Ga.]," Branch said. "He was a real close friend of my family, and when I tried out for the middle school team he kicked me off the bus because of my size. He was afraid I'd get hurt.

"He says today it didn't happen. Now you guys can help him regret it."

Branch's football career has consisted of overcoming near misses and misperceptions like that one. Concerns about his height have plagued him.

"At every level of football," Branch said, "I've been told I'm too small. But Louisville (his alma mater) and Coach Belichick were happy with me."

Branch was happiest the Pats didn't put him on injured reserve early in the season after hurting a knee in the second game at Arizona.

"I'm grateful to the coaches," Branch said. "They could have put me on IR. It was close."

Smart coaches don't waste good players. Belichick let Branch recover for half a season. He kind of got lost in the Pats' endless run of victories.

Smart quarterbacks don't forget guys who make catches. Tom Brady made Branch his top target when he returned Nov. 22 against the Chiefs.

"He can do so much with the ball after he gets it," Brady said. "He missed so much time, then came back and had a huge game in Kansas City. Except for Corey [Dillon], he was our top offensive weapon of the year."

Branch didn't make too much of his MVP award. Oh, he was happy and honored, and won't turn down the new car. But like every Patriot after a huge individual performance, he was a trifle sheepish, as if he won the vote only because some player had to. Why not Brady or Rodney Harrison instead of me, Branch wondered.

Any of five Pats, as usual, could have been named the outstanding individual contributor to their third Super Bowl win by three points.

That's their nature in a nutshell. But the voters didn't pick Branch by random. He made the plays that swung the game toward New England after a sloppy start.

"Not sloppy," Branch said. "Bad. We were awful in the first quarter."

After one first down in their first five possessions, the Pats began to solve the Eagles' shell game of blitzes. This left Branch in many favorable situations to make plays. On New England's scoring drives late in the second quarter and early in the third that gave them a 14-7 lead and swung the balance of the game in their favor, Branch had receptions of 27, 23, 21 and 19 yards.

"We did a great job of adjusting," Branch said. "I'm grateful, but this game shows it could have been any of us who were MVP."

With 21 catches in back-to-back Super Bowls, Branch seems to have a knack for his sport's biggest stage.

"All football players think that," he said.

Few football players have the knack, however. Branch does, whether or not he downplays it.

"I'm happiest that my kids and family were here to see us win," Branch said. "We'll go home to my sister's house here and have a small party. You're not invited."

Neither is anyone who once called Branch "Shorty."

—By Michael Gee, *Boston Herald*

Position: *Wide receiver*
Height: *5'9"*
Weight: *193*
Born: *7/18/79*
College: *Louisville*
NFL Experience: *3 years*

Nancy Lane/Boston Herald

OFFENSE

Passing

PLAYER	ATT	COMP	YDS	TD	INT
Tom Brady	474	288	3692	28	14
Rohan Davey	10	4	54	0	0
Adam Vinatieri	1	1	4	1	0

Rushing

PLAYER	ATT	YDS	TD
Corey Dillon	345	1635	12
Kevin Faulk	54	255	2
Patrick Pass	39	141	0
Cedric Cobbs	22	50	0
Tom Brady	43	28	0
Rabih Abdullah	13	13	1
Bethel Johnson	2	8	0
David Patten	1	5	0
Larry Izzo	1	0	0
Rohan Davey	4	-1	0

Receiving

PLAYER	REC	YDS	TD
David Givens	56	874	3
David Patten	44	800	7
Deion Branch	35	454	4
Daniel Graham	30	364	7
Kevin Faulk	26	248	1
Patrick Pass	28	215	0
Christian Fauria	16	195	2
Troy Brown	17	184	1
Bethel Johnson	10	174	1
Corey Dillon	15	103	1
Jed Weaver	8	93	0
Dan Klecko	3	18	0
Ben Watson	2	16	0
Rabih Abdullah	1	9	0
Mike Vrabel	2	3	2

SPECIAL TEAMS

Field Goals

PLAYER	1-29	20-29	30-39	40-49	50+
Adam Vinatieri	0/0	13/13	7/7	11/12	0/1

Punting

PLAYER	NO	AVG	INSIDE 20	LONG
Josh Miller	56	42.0	19	69

Punt Returns

PLAYER	RET	YARDS	AVG	TD
Kevin Faulk	20	133	6.7	0
Troy Brown	12	83	6.9	0
Bethel Johnson	4	8	2.0	0
Tyrone Poole	2	6	3.0	0
Deion Branch	1	0	0	0
Randall Gay	1	0	0	0

Kickoff Returns

PLAYER	RET	YDS	AVG	LONG	TD
Bethel Johnson	41	1016	24.8	93	1
Patrick Pass	6	115	19.2	24	0
Kevin Faulk	4	73	18.3	24	0
Kevin Kasper	3	61	20.3	21	0
Tully Banta-Cain	1	21	21.0	21	0
David Patten	1	16	16.0	16	0

DEFENSE

Tackles

PLAYER	TOTAL	SOLO	AST
Rodney Harrison	138	94	44
Tedy Bruschi	122	76	46
Ted Johnson	77	55	22
Mike Vrabel	71	54	17
Eugene Wilson	67	57	10
Willie McGinest	51	36	15
Ty Warren	48	38	10
Vince Wilfork	42	27	15
Roman Phifer	40	30	10
Richard Seymour	39	24	15
Asante Samuel	36	34	2
Randall Gay	34	29	5

Don Davis	32	20	12
Rosevelt Colvin	32	18	14
Keith Traylor	28	23	5
Ty Law	28	23	5
Tully Banta-Cain	28	18	10
Larry Izzo	25	22	3
Dexter Reid	23	15	8
Jarvis Green	21	15	6
Earthwind Moreland	17	15	2
Troy Brown	17	14	3
Tyrone Poole	13	12	1
Patrick Pass	11	11	0
Je'Rod Cherry	11	9	2
Rabih Abdullah	7	6	1
Dan Klecko	5	3	2
Kevin Kasper	5	4	1
David Givens	5	5	0
Steve Neal	4	4	0
Eric Alexander	3	3	0
Justin Kurpeikis	3	1	2
Adam Vinatieri	2	2	0
David Patten	2	2	0
Shawn Mayer	2	2	0
Daniel Graham	2	2	0
Tom Brady	2	2	0
Matt Chatham	2	2	0
Lonie Paxton	1	0	1
Dan Koppen	1	1	0
Ethan Kelley	1	1	0
Bethel Johnson	1	1	0
Kevin Faulk	1	1	0
Cedric Cobbs	1	1	0

Sacks

PLAYER	SACKS
Willie McGinest	9.5
Mike Vrabel	5.5
Richard Seymour	5
Rosevelt Colvin	5
Jarvis Green	4
Tedy Bruschi	3.5
Ty Warren	3.5
Rodney Harrison	3
Vince Wilfork	2
Roman Phifer	1.5
Tully Banta-Cain	1.5
Ted Johnson	1

Interceptions

PLAYER	NO	YDS	AVG	TD
Eugene Wilson	4	51	12	0
Troy Brown	3	22	7	0
Tedy Bruschi	3	70	23	0
Rodney Harrison	2	12	6	0
Randall Gay	2	23	11	0
Roman Phifer	1	26	26	0
Tyrone Poole	1	21	21	0
Asante Samuel	1	34	34	1
Tully Banta-Cain	1	4	4	0
Ty Law	1	0	0	0
Willie McGinest	1	27	27	0

TEAM

	Patriots	Opp		Patriots	Opp
Touchdowns	49	31	Total rushing yards	2134	1572
			Average per rush	4.1	3.9
First downs	344	290	Rushing TDs	15	9
Rushing	120	83			
Passing	193	177	Total passing yards	3588	3400
Penalty	31	30	Average per pass	7.73	6.90
			Passing TDs	29	18

	Patriots	Opp
Total offensive yards	5722	4972

Sports Publishing Congratulates the New England Patriots — 2005 Super Bowl Champions!

Celebrate with other titles from Sports Publishing perfect for any fan of Boston sports!

Lou Gorman: One Pitch from Glory
by Lou Gorman

- 6 x 9 hardcover
- 256 pages
- b/w photos throughout
- $24.95
- 2005 release!

More Tales from the Red Sox Dugout
by Bill Nowlin and Jim Prime

- 5.5 x 8.25 hardcover
- 200 pages
- photos throughout
- $19.95 (hardcover)
- $14.95 (softcover)

Ted Williams: The Pursuit of Perfection
by Bill Nowlin and Jim Prime

- 8.5 x 11 hardcover
- 200 pages
- b/w photos throughout
- Includes Audio CD!
- $39.95

Boston Red Sox: 2004 World Series Champions
by The Boston Herald

- 8.5 x 11 hard/trade paper
- 128 pages
- color photos throughout
- $19.95 (hardcover)
- $14.95 (trade paper)

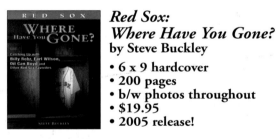
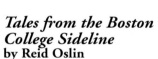

Red Sox: Where Have You Gone?
by Steve Buckley

- 6 x 9 hardcover
- 200 pages
- b/w photos throughout
- $19.95
- 2005 release!

Red Sox vs. Yankees: The Great Rivalry
by Harvey Frommer and Frederic Frommer

- 8.5 x 11 trade paper
- 256 pages
- photos throughout
- $14.95
- 2005 Release!

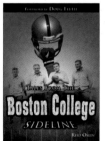

Tales from the Boston College Sideline
by Reid Oslin

- 5.5 x 8.25 hardcover
- 200 pages
- photos throughout
- $19.95

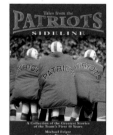

Tales from the Patriots Sideline
by Michael Felger

- 5.5 x 8.25 hardcover
- 200 pages
- photos throughout
- $19.95

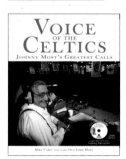

Voice of the Celtics: Johnny Most's Greatest Calls
by Mike Carey with Jamie Most

- 8.5 x 11 hardcover
- color photos throughout
- 160 pages • $29.95
- Includes audio CD!

High Above Courtside: The Lost Memoirs of Johnny Most
by Mike Carey with Jamie Most

- 6 x 9 hardcover
- 425 pages
- 8-page b/w photo section
- $24.95